Guardians of the Heart

The labyrinth of Minos imagined in Ottoman times
from Alain Manesson Mallet's *Description de L'Univers* (1685)

Mahmoud Shelton

Guardians of the Heart

Essays on Sacred Geography

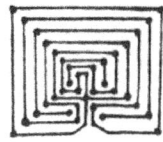

Temple of Justice Books

Copyright © 2022 D.M. Shelton

All rights reserved. This book or any portion thereof may not be reproduced or used in any manner whatsoever without the express written permission of the publisher.

Temple of Justice Books
templeofjustice@icloud.com

Printed in the United States of America
by Lightning Source Inc.

ISBN 978-0-9741468-4-3

Cover and maps by B.A.B.

Contents

Introduction   7

AMERICA

The Klamath Balance   11

The Modocs and a World's Heart   21

Some Remarks on the "Mystery Walls"   39

Racing Shadows   57

EUROPE

Idris in Wales   67

The Labyrinth of the Age of Gold   79

The Lost Ottoman Heart of Europe   97

The Place of Ivan Aguéli   117

Many arts are withheld from us because we have not ingratiated ourselves to God so that he would make them manifest to us. To make iron into copper is not as much as to make it into gold. Hence what is less God has allowed to emerge. What is more is still hidden up to the time of the arts of Elias when he will come.

Paracelsus

∇

Introduction

2021 marked the passing of a century since René Guénon, Shaykh `Abdul-Wahid Yahya, published his first book. The appearance of his *oeuvre* in its fullness constituted a providential counterbalance to the solidifying effects of materialism and subsequent psychic dissolution that has come to dominate the world. Among the less urgent aspects of his work, seemingly, is his elucidation of the principles of sacred geography; and while the concept of a sacred landscape may not be altogether unrecognized in the present day, attempts to understand are doomed to fall victim to these same effects of materialism and dissolution, that is, unless recourse is made to Guénon's writings.[1] Since the shaykh always preferred the principles of a subject over its secondary expressions, his focus was on the role of the supreme spiritual center rather than on the various secondary centers modeled upon it during the course of history. Among his favorite expressions for the spiritual center was "Heart of the World," a name applied to Jerusalem in the Abrahamic traditions. The supreme center must remain by definition inviolate, and so the city of Jerusalem that has suffered through this last century is

---

[1] As I have previously insisted, John Michell is among the very few authors on the subject to have made recourse to Guénon's writings, especially *Le Roi du Monde*.

not the supreme center. Indeed, the expression "World's Heart" is also known in Native American tradition, and what is indicated by this name is traditionally understood to apply at once to an inviolate source, the supreme center, as well as to its formulation on the landscape. There is a teaching likewise belonging to the Abrahamic traditions that is expressed in the words of the Holy Prophet of Islam: "There is an organ in the body that if healthy, the whole body is healthy, but if corrupted, the whole body is corrupted. Truly it is the heart." Given the traditional correspondence between the microcosm of the human form and the macrocosm of the world, the suffering of a world's heart concerns that entire world; and Jerusalem is not the only heart to have suffered attack.

  The following essays were conceived separately, and so are presented separately. Any of them may be read independently, but taken together, it will be found that they share themes relating to the composition of sacred landscapes and the methods by which they were safeguarded. The essays have been grouped in sections focusing on America and Europe respectively, with the former preceding the latter, contrary to the inherited notion that America is the New World. For the most part, these writings proceed from what has already been established in *The Red and the White: Perspectives on America and the Primordial Tradition*, and *Sacred Geography and the Paths of the Sun*. Here the topics emphasize matters of particular contemporary relevance, such as the Klamath water crisis on the California border: as the consequence of tactics employed during the invasion of Europeans, the Klamath Basin, as well as the life-giving river that flows from it, has been corrupted, to all appearances beyond the possibility of healing.

  Despite the present situation, we should not be hopeless. Hopelessness is a form of psychic dissolution far more harmful than any physical pandemic. I personally have taken comfort in sauntering upon the

Introduction

haunted lands I visit for the sake of research. For me, research has meant to "search again" for what has been forgotten. Thankfully, there are yet sources of traditional knowledge that offer healing to the microcosm and macrocosm alike, and René Guénon made it possible for the people of this time to identify them. Now that we have been shown, we hope to proceed with sincere steps (*qadama sidq*).

Mahmoud Shelton
Rajab 1443 / February 2022

AMERICA

∇

The Klamath Balance

Perhaps the defining characteristic of the early 21st century is the sharpening awareness that there are detrimental consequences resulting from humanity's disregard for nature. Of course, the Industrial Revolution gave rise to technologies that have made these consequences increasingly dire. While there is no ignoring the fact that these technologies developed in the Christian West, it should be observed that it was only with the demise of Christendom as a traditional world that materialism could dominate the Western worldview; and so materialistic science, freed from the sacred constraints of Christianity, could be employed to exploit nature for profane gain. Be that as it may, there is a worsening crisis in the American West that is emblematic of the consequences of such exploitation. This crisis concerns the survival of the Klamath River, and the global attention it has received is no doubt an indication of its vital significance in the efforts to confront worsening ecological imbalance.

The Klamath River is one of the principal settings for the lifecycle of the anadromous salmon, and one of only three natural routes through the volcanic Cascade Range that stretches through the Pacific Northwest.[2] For

---

[2] The other two are the Pit River - in actuality the principal source of the Sacramento River that figures so prominently in

these reasons alone, its vital importance to the traditional cultures of the region should be obvious. Present controversies swirl over dwindling water resources, and the conflicting claims on those resources of two communities: farmers at the river's source in the Klamath Basin, and the native Yuroks ("Downriver" people) at the mouth of the Klamath whose culture is inextricably bound to the river and its salmon. Over time, however, it has become clear to both parties that they have a shared interest in the health of the Klamath waters, and for this reason have come together to work towards the removal of four of the five dams along the river's upper reaches. Besides presenting insurmountable obstacles to migrating salmon, the constricting of the river has ensured the accumulation of sediment and poisons from upriver farming, as well as increased temperatures that allow for the growth of deadly pathogens. No doubt the construction of the dams was a monstrous folly, since the hydroelectric power they were designed to provide has proven to be a bad economic investment, ultimately at the cost of the life of the river. It is telling that despite the cooperation of the people directly involved, the dams still have not come down, and that there remains a resistance to their removal among those with a blind faith in modern industrial development.

  While the damming of the Klamath is an error that may yet be undone, there is a truth that is even harder to face. The establishment of farming in the Klamath Basin was facilitated through a massive reclamation project at the turn of the last century that involved the draining of some 80 percent of the region's wetlands. Modern science has come to understand the general importance of wetlands in purifying water, and even in reducing the environmental damage traced to industrial

---

the agricultural economy - and the Columbia River, the "Great River" of the West (to which the name "Oregon" somehow relates) that was formerly hoped to be the long-sought Northwest Passage.

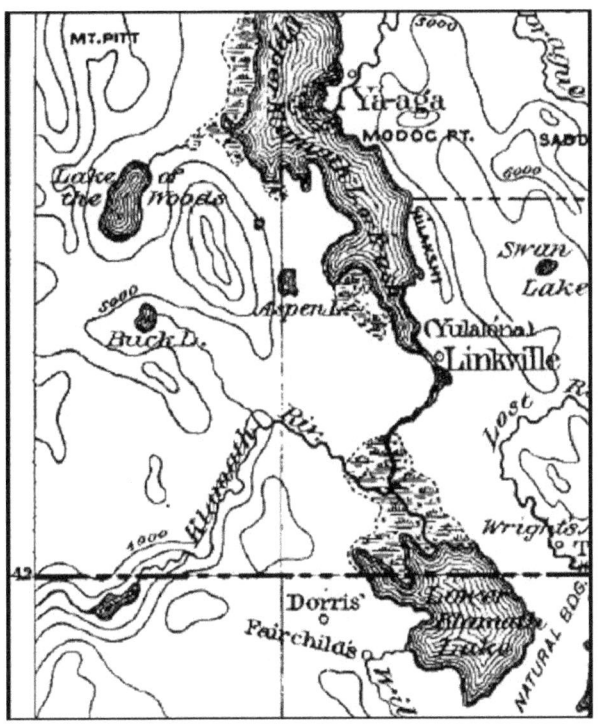

emissions.[3] Specifically, the consequences of draining the Klamath Basin are perhaps best expressed in the current characterization of the Klamath as "a river upside-down,"[4] since the river is wilder and cleaner at its mouth than at its source. To understand this inversion, reference must be made to the original landscape of the Klamath River's headwaters (above)[5]. It may be seen that the

---

[3] The use of the expression "draining the swamp" persists in a positive sense in the English language, betraying a belief in the superiority of modern industry over nature.
[4] Russ Rymer, "Reuniting a River," *National Geographic Magazine*, December 2008.
[5] Detail from the "Map of the Headwaters of the Klamath River" by Albert S. Gatschet (*The Klamath Indians of Southwestern*

Klamath River formerly proceeded from a balance of lakes, the Upper and the Lower Klamath in Oregon and California respectively, that were joined by the Link River through Linkville, now Klamath Falls. The Upper Klamath Lake yet exists, whereas the Lower Klamath Lake – once known as Big Klamath Lake - has been all but obliterated, so an imbalance is immediately apparent. As for the Link River, it still exists in name, but it no longer links to the Lower Klamath Lake; and there is an even more significant manner in which its function has been altered by the Klamath Project.

An 1885 article from "The American Antiquarian" includes an account of a most remarkable curiosity that originally belonged to the Link River:

> ...and that is that it is occasionally blown dry. This must seem astounding to our readers, but such is the fact. It is caused by a steady wind blowing from the south and up the river – this through a seemingly canyon – and the waters of Big Klamath Lake roll up towards the north, and the water is literally all blown down toward the northern end of the lake, and there being but a shallow outlet into Link river, and the water being blown up the lake, leaves no water, and so the river runs dry. The shallow outlet of Big Klamath Lake has been caused by the aforesaid Indians, who wish to confine the waters of the lake for the sake of the tule lands.[6]

Oregon, part I, Washington: Government Printing Office, 1890, page ii).

[6] William J. Clarke, "Rock Piles and Ancient Dams in the Klamath Valley," *The American Antiquarian*, 1885, accessed from Tom Doty's invaluable website (www.dotycoyote.com).

The method of confining the waters involved stone structures that the author describes as the ruins of dams, "evidence of a race of people, of whom the present Indians at Klamath know nothing, who inhabited the Klamath Lake country many years ago;" and while he insists that the Indians "claim no knowledge of the formations of these dams," an article appearing in the same publication a few years prior indicates quite otherwise. In "Mythologic Text of the Klamath Language of Southern Oregon" from 1879, Albert Gatschet refers to the creation of the world by the principal figure Kmúkamtch, the "Old Man of the ancients," and includes the following detail: "Hereupon he also ordered that at Cascade Falls (Linkville) a rock-dam should come into existence; that when the south wind blows, it should drive back the waters, loudly roaring at their rushing down, and that the Indians should then, on the dry river bottom, gather up the fish and feed on them."[7]

In keeping with this "astounding" behavior of the Link River, then, the stone structures were traditionally understood to have a divine origin, and the people "of whom the present Indians of Klamath know nothing" were in fact well-known in mythology.[8] Modernity belittles myths as puerile attempts by primitive people to understand everyday phenomena, whereas here we are confronted with a phenomenon which modern science cannot comprehend. As for the traditional science that would seem to be at work here, safeguarding the wetlands while providing harvests of

---

[7] www.dotycoyote.com
[8] In Biblical terms, the parting of the waters in the Klamath Basin might be compared with the parting of the Red Sea by Moses in the book of Genesis. Despite the agreement of these independent eyewitness reports on the purpose of the Link River's rock structures, modern experts would prefer to categorize the "dams" as mundane "fish weirs" (cf. Theodore Stern, "The Trickster in Klamath Mythology," *Western Folklore*, volume 12, number 3, July 1953, page 165).

fish, it involved the workings of wind and water specifically, and so it is worth recalling the Chinese designation of traditional geomancy as Feng Shui, literally "wind water." As suggestive as this association is, the function of the stone structures remains a mystery, since they were swept away by a science applied to maximize agricultural productivity in the Klamath Basin, as the 1885 article anticipated: "There is a movement on foot to remove these obstructions at the mouth of Link river. Such being done would decrease the depth of the lake a foot or so, and make thousands of acres of land arable that are nothing but tule."

There is a principle called "Chesterton's Fence" that is particularly apt here, especially since its literal meaning is more relevant to the present context than the political milieu in which it is most commonly applied. The principle is named for its author G.K. Chesterton, who describes the example of a fence or gate across a road:

> The more modern type of reformer goes gaily up to it and says, "I don't see the use of this; let us clear it away." To which the more intelligent type of reformer will do well to answer: "If you don't see the use of it, I certainly won't let you clear it away. Go away and think. Then, when you can come back and tell me that you do see the use of it, I may allow you to destroy it."[9]

Just like the fence upon the road, the dam upon the Link River was cleared away without a proper understanding of its use, as were the wetlands it was designed to safeguard. In both cases, agriculture was the justification for destruction, although scientists are now coming to

---

[9] *The Thing: Why I am a Catholic*, 1929.

understand that agriculture may not be a viable option for the drought-ravaged Klamath Basin after all.[10]

    The alternation of the flow of water in the Link River from north to south and from south to north must have been an incomparable display of equilibrium. With the Upper and Lower Klamath Lakes like the pans of a set of scales,[11] the traditional geography of the region demonstrated a subtle balance that was the source of the Klamath River. Broken through human agency, its present state may in turn give the lie to belittling human responsibility for the current ecological crisis. At the same time, it is important to acknowledge that the original balance of the basin incorporated an artificial element, at least in the form of stone dams that even in a ruined state preserved the health of the wetlands. The removal of this element has transformed the Klamath River that flows from the basin into a river "upside down," and the five modern dams constricting the river parody traditional geomancy through the harm they have caused.[12]

---

[10] Concerning the chronic drought conditions, it is no accident that a ritual specialty of Native culture along the Klamath River is the use of "Rain Rocks" to control the weather. On the Rain Rock unearthed at Gottsville, see *The Red and the White: Perspectives on America and the Primordial Tradition*, Temple of Justice Books, 2019, chapter 6. Here is no doubt another example of a supernatural element essential to maintaining the balance of the Klamath, and even though such stones have survived, it is doubtful that their use is fully understood. Along the Klamath at least, the crisis of Climate Change arises in the absence of changing the climate for the better.

[11] It may be noted that the north-south axis is polar, and that the Scales was once a polar rather than a zodiacal constellation. See *Sacred Geography and the Paths of the Sun*, Temple of Justice Books, 2021, page 99.

[12] That there are *five* dams choking the river is itself a parody of the sacred significance of the number five that is specific to the traditional cultures of the region. See *The Red and the White*, chapter 7.

If it is offered that a balance may have finally been attained between the farmers and the Yuroks, any commendable harmony between them still ignores the imbalance that is the real source of their suffering; and besides, the interests of both are often enough opposed by the Klamath Indians who seek to preserve the ecology of the Upper Klamath Lake alone. With due respect to the dignity of all involved, there is no equivalence between the ancient Yurok understanding of their primordial responsibility over creation and the farmers' hope to preserve a modern way of life created by the government and forced upon the region's ecology. Very significantly, it is the ancient fulcrum of the Klamath balance that is specifically plagued by unrest, as protests and lawless acts in support of farming are focused at the headgates of the A Canal.

In the meantime, the salmon die in record numbers. In a recent news report, a Yurok representative mused on the state of things: "We're supposed to be the stewards of this land, the connection to the salmon; most of us have spent our careers fighting for this river…It takes a toll…when we see what's happening, and we don't know if there's anything that can be done about it."[13] No doubt the damage is from a certain point of view irreparable. Dams may yet be taken down, and nature might even be restored at the expense of the agricultural industry, but the knowledge of how to restore the mysterious workings of the Link River belongs, as we have seen, to a supernatural domain. There is, however, a reminder that matters are not hopeless, since according to the Native view, the "Old Man of the ancients" will ultimately awaken from his bed in the Klamath Basin, and restore the world as it was when it was made.[14] In the

---

[13] "No Water, No Life: Running Out of Water on the California-Oregon Border," *The Guardian* website, 1 July 2021.
[14] See *Sacred Geography and the Paths of the Sun*, page 108.

Native view, the Klamath balance will one day be restored.

Guardians of the Heart

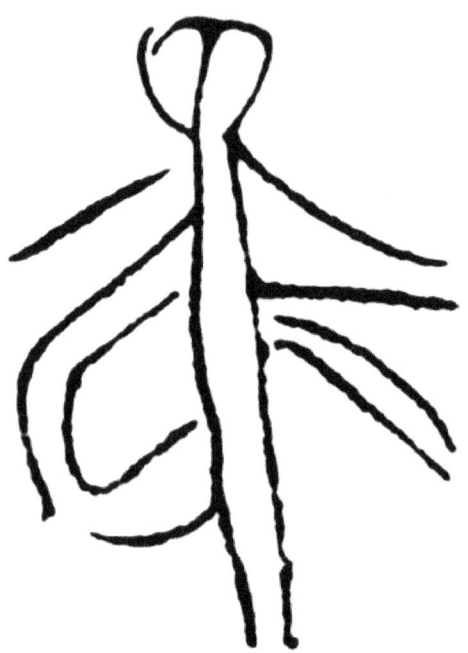

∇

The Modocs and a World's Heart

The contemporary focus on the water crisis in the Klamath Basin is not the first time the region has attracted global attention. The Modoc Wars of the second half of the 19th century were very widely publicized,[15] and they bear remembering today, not least since the destruction of the Klamath ecological balance followed so close upon this conflict. The destruction of the Modoc people proved to be among the last and bloodiest of the American military campaigns against its traditional civilization, as well as being the only campaign during which an American general was slain. The total remaking of the Klamath Basin by the American victors may well have been an expression of a vindictive resolve; and now more than a century after the spoils went to the victors, it would appear that "spoiling" has become the operative term regarding its geography. As for the Modocs, the tragedy they suffered would be difficult to exaggerate. In the words of the eyewitness and authority on traditional America Stephen Powers: "They fought with unparalleled heroism for their homes, but were crushed by superior power; and their fallen chiefs were held to a

---

[15] When poet Joaquin Miller published his account of his experience with the Shasta people who were the Modoc's immediate neighbors to the west, he chose the title *Life Amongst the Modocs* because of the public's familiarity with that name.

stern and awful accountability to laws which they had no hand or voice in making, and whose spirit and substance had been as wantonly violated by the conquering race as by themselves."[16]

The Modoc traditionally favored the "pellucid, fresh, and wholesome waters"[17] of what came to be known as the Lost River. Accordingly, the first of the wars leading to their removal was known as the Battle of Lost River in 1872. The perceived need to remove the Modocs was in fact driven by a land grabbing scheme belonging to but two men, the cattle baron Jesse Carr – dubbed by a contemporary journalist as "King of Squatters" - and Jesse Applegate of the famous pioneer family. Strategically, the "Two Jesses" planned to take control of the waters of the Klamath Basin at the expense of all others and in disregard of the law, as a recent account of the Modoc Wars has made clear after long being downplayed.[18] If their ill-advised ambition to do "nothing less than replumb the region's entire water system, damming rivers and draining lakes in the heart of the Modocs' traditional territory"[19] seems familiar, it is because the Klamath Project of the 20th century is but the legitimized fulfillment of their corrupt plan. The destruction of Modoc life is not excused by "manifest destiny;" it was the consequence of an invasion opposed to tradition[20] and the natural order. Today's water crisis is inextricably bound up with the Modoc catastrophe.

The author of *Spirit in the Rock* insists that the diversion of the Lost River and the draining of Tule Lake

---

[16] *Tribes of California*, Berkeley: University of California Press, 1976, page 266.
[17] Ibid. page 255.
[18] Jim Compton, *Spirit in the Rock: The Fierce Battle for Modoc Homelands*, Pullman: Washington State University Press, 2017.
[19] Ibid., page 67.
[20] There is no question here of the Two Jesses representing the Christian tradition, despite their shared Biblical name, since greed is among the Seven Deadly Sins.

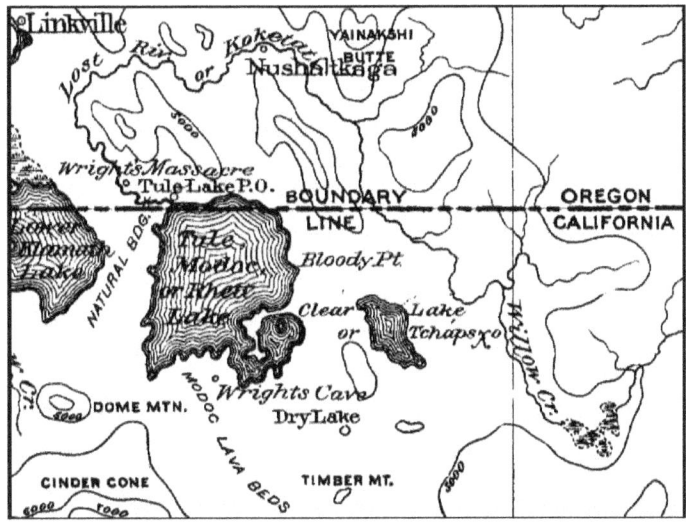

Heart of the Modoc Lands[21]

"cut out the heart of the Modocs' traditional territories and destroyed the center of their spiritual universe." Indeed, as I have noted elsewhere,[22] the designation "Tule" for the lake is sometimes rendered "Tula," and René Guénon has identified the latter term as a name of the supreme spiritual center; Tula then came to be applied to so many secondary centers modelled upon the supreme center. Where the Lost River flowed into Tule Lake, a natural stone bridge joined the opposing banks of the river, but this unifying bridge was a casualty of the Klamath Project.[23] Another feature of the Modoc "spiritual universe" was the reported presence of ancient

---

[21] Detail from the "Map of the Headwaters of the Klamath River" by Albert S. Gatschet (op. cit.).

[22] See *The Red and the White: Perspectives on America and the Primordial Tradition*, page 18.

[23] See Compton, page 28 for juxtaposing images of the natural bridge and the modern dam that replaced it.

stone constructions: "All that remains are the ruins of dams, one of which is located on Link River, within a stone's throw of Linkville, and a number of others, notably, one on Lost River."[24] It would appear that this assertion from 1885 has never since been investigated. Today, the ruins on the Link River no longer exist – another victim, apparently, of the Klamath Project – yet there is still a network of linear stone constructions at the source of the Lost River near its confluence with Willow Creek in the eastern Modoc lands. Somewhat like a dam,[25] the network runs in places into the waters of today's Clear Lake Reservoir, though this may simply suggest that it antedates the modern Clear Lake Dam. The unmortared stone network is accounted for today as the so-called "China Wall" of Jesse Carr.

However, if Carr's "China Wall" enclosed – illegally - some 84,000 acres as is claimed,[26] it is obvious from what remains that stone formed only part of its structure. What is more, the stone constructions are not continuous but begin and end without apparent reason in a meandering course through the landscape. Simply put, the stone network never enclosed anything, that is, until the addition of extensive sections of wood and wire that were necessary to connect the stone segments and present a barrier for livestock. Jesse Carr may have employed Chinese laborers among others, but any further association with China is far less concrete. Predictably, since the Great Wall of China is the best-known example of an exotic wall, the strange course and remarkable extent of this project is attributed to the "inscrutable" and industrious Chinese; even a story of a Chinese worker's

---

[24] William J. Clarke, op. cit. On the Link River, see "The Klamath Balance."
[25] Although Clarke uses the word "dam," since the construction he describes in the Link River was sometimes submerged, he also uses the word "wall." Of course, care should be taken in the use of terms which assume function.
[26] Compton, page 70.

burial beneath Carr's wall and his ghostly apparition would seem to be patterned on the macabre stories of workers buried within the Great Wall.[27] There are also very similar stone constructions far in the west of Modoc territory, upon a ridge near the source of Hot Creek, and though these have no name, their presence does accord with the statement from 1885 referring to "a number of others." It would seem, in any case, that Jesse Carr not only seized control of the waters of the Klamath Basin, but repurposed some of its stone constructions, or cairns, as well.

    Another indication that these cairns belong properly to the Native tradition emerges from the Modocs' last stand in 1873. Encouraged by the doctrines of the Ghost Dance,[28] some 50 Modoc warriors held out for months against a force ultimately ten times that number in the labyrinthine lava formations south of Tule Lake, in a place known as "Captain Jack's Stronghold" after their leader. Today there are remnants of stone barriers erected by the besieging army, and while the defenders had chosen a place naturally suited for their purpose, there are examples of stone structures built by the Modoc as well. Unlike the American army constructions, however, a cairn within the Stronghold forms a sort of wall too low to serve as an effective shield against artillery. Now, it was reported that the Modoc medicine man Curley-Headed Doctor employed magical methods to fortify the Stronghold, including three medicine flags and an encircling red rope of tule, and it is

---

[27] See Lee Juillerat, "Carr's Wall of China a Sight to See," *Herald and News*, Klamath Falls, Oregon, 23 January 2014. The report mentions an archaeologist's surprise in finding no trash heaps associated with such a massive construction project.

[28] According to Powers (op. cit., page 260), "the Modoc were led into their last terrible outbreak by belief that their dead were about to be restored to life and come to their assistance, and at the same time the Americans would be swallowed up in the earth."

certainly plausible that in the absence of any apparent physical utility, the meandering cairn at the Stronghold belongs to such methods.[29] Given the very comparable structures in the "China Wall" near Willow Creek, it may be significant that following his retreat from the Stronghold, Captain Jack sought refuge at Willow Creek before he was captured.

∇

Elsewhere I had occasion to mention a significant landform in the sacred geography of Tule Lake, Gmukamp's Bed.[30] Now known as Petroglyph Point and part of the Lava Beds National Monument, this was formerly a peninsula on the lake's southeastern edge, but the Klamath Project has exposed the surrounding lakebed. As its present name indicates, the base of the peninsula's sheer western face is covered in ancient petroglyphs which appear to have been made from reaching the cliff by boat.[31] Aside from contributing to the worsening water crisis, the draining of Tule Lake has had another miserable consequence, as wind-driven sands

---

[29] Cf. Compton, page 105. Even though these cairns have a tangible existence, their purpose remains of course obscure in the absence of a living tradition, just as the red tule rope used by Curley-Headed Doctor would appear as just a rope without the contemporary report that it served the Modoc defenders as "the line of death." Perhaps it goes without saying that the ones with the knowledge of such things – the leaders of the defense at the Stronghold – are silent, since the four were hanged and their corpses beheaded, with their heads sent east and only recently recovered (Compton, pages 245-8).
[30] *Sacred Geography and the Paths of the Sun*, page 108.
[31] Here the ancient boats included sailboats, evidently, since these are depicted among the petroglyphs.

from the exposed lakebed are wearing away the ancient messages in stone.

Among the markings there is a prominent glyph (page 20) that has been adopted by the National Park Service as an unofficial logo for the monument, and though it is featured on Park merchandise, its significance is nowhere considered. Thankfully, the publication of a paper by Arlene Benson and Floyd Buckskin provides a wealth of traditional knowledge relating to this motif in the context of another sacred site, designated "Modoc 75" and located in the eastern Modoc lands. The authors of the study are not Modoc, yet Floyd Buckskin is the custodian of a living tradition, that of the Achumawi or Pit River Indians neighboring the Modoc to the south. For this reason, Buckskin was able to identify an important pictograph at Modoc 75 (page 30): "Without prior knowledge of the panel and without any prompting, Buckskin suggested that the triangular motif at the top of the panel represents the World's Heart in his sky lodge, and that the circular motifs below may symbolize social groups or geographical locations." The authors cite the traditional doctrine transmitted by John P. Harrington: "Supreme Intelligence is vested in World's Heart, who resides in the middle of the world." With respect to Modoc tradition, Benson and Buckskin conclude that the panel depicts the Modoc Sky Chief "based on its bifurcated form and its position above, in the sky, and below, on Mount Shasta."[32] Now, it would appear that the prominent petroglyph at Gmukamp's Bed with its comparable bifurcated element is another representation of the same doctrine. There is more, however: the petroglyph (highlighted on page 29) is framed by a contour of the cliff that appears to have been deliberately shaped. Without a doubt the precise positioning of the

---

[32] Benson and Buckskin, "Modoc 75," *Rock Art Papers, Volume 2*, edited by Ken Hedges, San Diego Museum Papers no. 18, San Diego: San Diego Museum of Man, 1985, pages 136-7. The "sky lodge" is specifically associated with a triangular asterism.

Guardians of the Heart

The Modocs and a World's Heart

glyph is an example of what is known as rock art incorporation, that is, when peculiarities of the rock on which the glyph appears are relevant to the glyph itself. In this case, the frame is a mirror image of Mount Shasta that is clearly visible to the southwest, indeed along the azimuth of the winter solstice sunset (page 28).

In his incomparable writings on traditional symbolism, René Guénon favors the expression "Heart of the World" for the spiritual center that he derives from the Judeo-Christian tradition, a matter of some irony in this context. In a series of articles entitled "The Heart and the Cave," "The Mountain and the Cave," and "The Heart and the World Egg,"[33] he elucidates the profound meanings of these related symbols, many of which are relevant here. For example, the cave like the heart may be symbolized by the downturned triangle and be represented within the upward pointing triangle of the mountain, a precise configuration that is depicted at Tule Lake. Concerning the related symbol of the World Egg, Guénon indicates the following:

> ...in fact, the "World Egg" is central in relation to the "cosmos" and, at the same time contains in seed form all that the latter will contain in its fully manifested state...The two halves into which the "World Egg" is divided according to one

---

[33] These articles have been collected by Michel Vâlsan in *Symbols of Sacred Science* (Hillsdale: Sophia Perennis, 2004).

The Modocs and a World's Heart

of the most common aspects of its symbolism, become respectively heaven and earth.[34]

Elsewhere he mentions that such a division is "figured very clearly in the Far Eastern symbol of the *yin-yang*, which is itself not unrelated to the 'World Egg.'"[35] Guénon may have in mind the *yin-yang* formulation most familiar to modern readers, but if we consider another version that forms part of the "Chart of the Great Ultimate. (*Taiji tu*)" (at right), an unexpected comparison appears.

Here the division of *yang* and *yin*, or Heaven and Earth, in the top element corresponds to the bifurcated top elements representing World's Heart with its two identities, at once in the sky above and in the mountain below.[36] There is obviously significant

---

[34] "The Cave and the World Egg."
[35] "The Heart and the World Egg."
[36] In particular, the expression "Heart of the World" emphasizes this two-fold presence that the center contains, in a manner corresponding to the human heart. The heart contains both transcendent principle and worldly identity, the "two who have entered into the cave" or the two birds "abiding in the same tree." Ultimately "they are really one, the distinction between them being no more than illusory" (cf. Guénon, "The Heart and the Cave"), but this realization belongs only to the Supreme Identity, Harrington's "Supreme Intelligence." In cosmogonic terms, Guénon relates the Heart of the World prior to this differentiation to the *Rūh muhammadiyyah* of Islamic esoterism ("The Heart and the World Egg").

variation between the other elements in the Modoc 75 pictograph and those of the Tule Lake petroglyph,[37] but the arrangement of circles in the former may be compared to the Chinese chart, even in the number of circles. The five labeled circles in the chart depict the five phases, commonly called elements, that proceed from the union of *yin* and *yang*. These phases are also associated in traditional China with the Five Deities, or rather Five Forms of the Highest Deity, while in Achumawi cosmology, there are five Chiefs without parentage who appear in existence after World's Heart.[38] Admittedly, this emphasis on the number 5 is a general point of agreement between the Chinese tradition and that of the American Indians in this region, yet the specific comparisons linking these traditional worlds are too many to ignore. Ancient China was well aware of America, or Fusang, whereas a story of Fusang was told by the Shasta people, the immediate neighbors of the Modoc.[39] The earliest authority Stephen Powers was convinced of an ancient Chinese presence in California and defended his position with careful scholarship, but when the American government published his magnum opus, this material was censored. Regardless, it is worth recalling here that the name Fusang for America literally refers to the wondrous solar tree that was believed to be found there, since the images of the World's Heart do likewise suggest a stylized tree.

The most infamous link between the Far East and the lands of the Modoc remains the internment of Japanese Americans in the concentration camp at Tule Lake, or the Tule Lake War Relocation Center, during the

---

[37] If the circles in the former do indicate geographical locations, as Buckskin suggested, perhaps the lines in the latter petroglyph – and especially its central axis - indicate pathways.

[38] Istet Woiche, *Annikadel: The History of the Universe as Told by the Achumawi Indians of California*, Tucson: University of Arizona Press, 1992, page 6.

[39] On this subject, see *The Red and the White*, especially chapter 7.

Second World War. Yet even concerning the Japanese, there is a curious traditional connection to be observed between the Henwas of the Klamath Basin – shaped stones with the power of independent movement – and the Haniwas of ancient Japan, that likewise were figurines, albeit made from clay, that were held to be containers for souls. Leaving aside speculations on how such similarities came to be, it is worth insisting that the examples of the Chinese Wall and the Japanese internment camp are modern mockeries of an ancient bond that is mysterious.[40]

∇

A recent history of the Lava Beds National Monument published by the government bears the insightful title, *Center of the World, Edge of the World*. Clearly the setting of the Modoc Wars, in the American view, was at the limit of western expansion, and so at the "edge of the world." Curiously, this setting also straddles the 42nd parallel of latitude, that is, the historic line that marked the border between the ambitions of the Spanish and Mexicans in turn, and the so-called Oregon Territory of British and American interests. Of course, the conquest of Modoc lands was accomplished by representatives of the latter. Originally, against the Papal sanctification of their rivals, the British Empire had found justification for its American ambitions in an antecedent and therefore superior claim deriving from the legendary voyages of a 12th century Welsh prince. The supposed American

---

[40] To these examples should be added the very recent influx into the Shasta Valley of Hmong people, whose culture suggests an ancient meeting of East and West, and who reportedly recognize the sacredness of the landscape through their traditional geomancy.

evidence for these expeditions was two-fold: there were persistent rumors of "Welsh Indians" of light complexion who understood that Celtic language, yet whose existence on the western frontier proved elusive; and there was the discovery of abandoned stone "forts" that recalled for the British Americans the castles of Wales. The author of the definitive work on the legend quotes Bernard DeVoto: "'In the United States, it became our most elaborate historical myth and exercised a direct influence on our history.'"[41]

It is therefore worth recognizing here that the name of the medieval Welsh prince was "Madoc," a name that is strangely similar to the name "Modoc." We have already recognized mysterious Far Eastern elements in the Modoc landscape, and here a strange echo of a western legend appears.[42] Obviously east and west only have meaning in relation to a place of reference. We have seen that in the light of Native tradition, Tule Lake and Mount Shasta testify to an identification with the center of the world, or rather its heart. If a center is a place of balance, is it so incredible that traces of the East are mirrored there alongside those of the West, since the

---

[41] Gwyn A. Williams, *Madoc: The Legend of the Welsh Discovery of America*, Oxford: Oxford University Press, 1979, page 31.

[42] A relationship between the Chinese and Celtic forms has in fact already been considered by René Guénon: "It is at least curious to note the singular resemblance between the name and title of Yü the Great and those of *Hu Gadarn* in Celtic tradition; should we suppose from this that they are something like secondary and particular 'localizations' of one and the same 'prototype,' which goes back much further, perhaps even to the primordial tradition itself?" (*The Great Triad*, Hillsdale: Sophia Perennis, 2001, page 99) Furthermore, if the role of Hu Gadarn is comparable to that of Yü the Great, who brings order to the land and waters after the Flood, so too is that of Gmukamp, who dives into the waters to form the land from handfuls of earth (cf. "Where the Sun and Moon Live" in Thomas Doty, *Doty Meets Coyote*, Ashland: Blackstone, 2016) and who builds the "dams" on the Link River.

World's Heart must reconcile no less than Heaven and Earth?

In *The Red and the White*, I observed that the notion of Welsh or White Indians coincided with Native accounts of an ancient renewal overseen by Hyperborean representatives of the Primordial Tradition. As a consequence, Native memory of an "ancient white people" was interpreted as proof of the Madoc legend. Even when considered separately, however, the search for the "Lost Brothers" of Wales uncannily mirrored the hope of various Native tribes for the return of their "Lost White Brothers."[43] As for their trace upon the landscape, the stone structures that were perceived as medieval fortifications were nothing of the sort. At Fort Mountain in Georgia, for example, there is presently a plaque commemorating the attribution of its "fortifications" to Prince Madoc. Yet these "fortifications" are meandering low walls of unmortared stone that are, in fact, disconnected, which for a number of reasons "have no apparent strategic value whatever."[44] These would be better identified as linear cairns, and so could naturally be compared with those in evidence in Modoc lands.

By the time of the Modoc Wars, however, thoughts of Madoc had apparently been forgotten. The cairns of Modoc lands were not even attributed to the vanquished – nor indeed to the "Welsh Indians" - but rather destroyed or adapted for strategies of exploitation with hardly a thought at all. The petroglyphs of Gmukamp's Bed were also ofttimes attributed to others, but in light of the Madoc legend, it is significant that some symbols have been identified as Druidic.[45] Now, it is

---

[43] See *The Red and the White*, page 79. Immediate neighbors of the Modocs, the Paiute shared this doctrine (see Sarah Winnemucca Hopkins, *Life Among the Paiutes*, Boston, 1883, pages 5-7).
[44] Philip E. Smith, "Aboriginal Stone Constructions in the Southern Piedmont," 1962.
[45] Ryan Bartholomew, "The Petroglyphs: History or Hype?," *Klamath County Historical Society Trumpeter*, number 109,

important to recognize that the Celtic tradition, of which the Druids were the proper custodians, was, like the American Indian tradition, the result of an ancient renewal resulting from the fusion of Hyperborean and Atlantean forms.[46] These traditions are certainly analogous, but not identical. Their reconciliation is comprehensible, however, by referring to the Hyperborean or northern current that inspired alike the traditions belonging to the "Welsh" and "Indians."

As a representative of another analogous tradition, that of the Classical world, the Roman poet Virgil in his Fourth Ecologue relates a prophecy of the return of the Golden Age that belongs properly to the Hyperborean or Primordial Tradition. In keeping with this, the return of the Golden Age is linked to the "reign of Apollo," whose Hyperborean identity is explicit. In Celtic lands, cosmic restoration is fixed upon the figure of the "once and future king" Arthur, whose name means bear, and who was in fact associated with the northern constellation of the Bear, or "Arthur's Wain." Throughout Britain, tales were told of the king being in undying slumber under hills from which he would one day emerge,[47] not unlike a bear that hibernates, and most often these hills are located in Wales.[48] In Modoc lands, the designation "Gmukamp's Bed" refers to a very comparable situation:

---

summer 2015. The author reproduces an article from 1929, and so provides the proper source of the Druidic attribution that would be reproduced nearly verbatim in 1931 by Wishar S. Cerve in *Lemuria: Lost Continent of the Pacific*. This is not an isolated example, however, and may be compared with the modern obsession with perceiving Ogham in Native American petroglyphs.

[46] See *The Red and the White*, chapter 2.

[47] On the comparable Classical theme of the emperor *vivit et non vivit*, cf. *Sacred Geography and the Paths of the Sun*, page 77.

[48] Rather remarkably in the present context, the name Madoc even appears in Welsh legend as a brother of King Arthur.

> Someday Kamookumputs[49] will surely wake up and look out over the world he made. He may be angry at how things have changed and bring the water back to cover Tule Lake again, changing the world to be like it was when he first made it.[50]

Moreover, since Gmukamp is literally the "Old Man of the ancients," his role in restoring his world's "first" condition recalls the Classical association of Saturn with the Golden Age.

There is a further point to be made here, however. For Virgil, who calls the Golden Age the Age of Saturn, its restoration nevertheless involves Apollo, whose influence belongs to a more recent period. Similarly, King Arthur was an historic and not prehistoric leader; moreover, the historical formulation of the "Matter of Britain" actually involved three principal elements: a legendary foundation that is Celtic, an obvious setting that is Christian, and motifs relating to Islamic esoterism. Now, in Modoc mythology, Gmukamp's closest companion is named Aisis, and at least as early as 1877, this figure was explicitly identified with Jesus, ostensibly "on account of a phonetic similarity between the names."[51] Regardless, traditional mythology must be true for all time, and it should be observed that in the Arthurian and Modoc examples alike, there is an Abrahamic presence that must participate in the

---

[49] This name has been spelled with a great many variations, and we have chosen to use the simplest, if not necessarily the most correct.

[50] Cited in the pamphlet "Petroglyph Point: An Interpretive Walk" published by Lava Beds National Monument and Lava Beds Natural History Association. Cf. "Where Koomookumpts Sleeps" in Doty, op. cit.

[51] Albert S. Gatschet, op. cit., page xciv.

restoration of the primordial condition, despite Christians of British descent having been involved in the Modoc genocide.

The tragic implications of this involvement are clear: people who appeared white failed to recognize the Modoc as their "lost brothers," and so in turn failed to be the "white brothers" of Native lore. In Arthurian legend, Parzival of Wales is expected at the castle of his kinsman at Montsalvasche, a place near the rising place of the Sun that is "at one and the same time the 'sacred isle' and the 'polar mountain'" and so easily identified with the Terrestrial Paradise.[52] Montsalvasche is above all the home of the Grail, symbol of the heart par excellence,[53] and so it serves as the Arthurian Heart of the World. When Parzival first arrives, he fails to ask the right question, and so the legendary wasteland will not be healed until he is sent out from this place and ultimately returns with the requisite understanding. No doubt the heart of the Modoc world will never be healed until the American failure is properly recognized.

In Memoriam Thomas Doty

---

[52] René Guénon, *The King of the World*, Hillsdale: Sophia Perennis, 2001, page 32.

[53] The Grail is even to be identified with the Heart of Jesus; see Guénon's "The Sacred Heart and the Legend of the Holy Grail" in *Symbols of Sacred Science* (op. cit.). There is also a clear analogue of the Grail in Modoc mythology, the "disk" of Gmukamp (cf. Jeremiah Curtin, *Myths of the Modocs*, Boston: Little, Brown and Company, 1912, page 381); it has been suggested that this disk is represented as a circular design in Modoc rock writing (cf. Don Hamm and Gordon Bettles, "House of the Rising Sun," *Talking With the Past: The Ethnography of Rock Art*, edited by Keyser et al., Portland: Oregon Archaeological Society, 2006).

∇

Some Remarks on the "Mystery Walls"

In addressing aspects of the Klamath water crisis,[54] I have referred to the ancient "dams" or "walls" of the Klamath Basin, including the so-called "China Wall" attributed to the cattle baron Jesse Carr. These stone structures might better be described as "linear cairns,"[55] and since such structures are not restricted to this region, a separate investigation is called for. The example of Carr's "China Wall" is helpful when evaluating other examples of such cairns, however, and not least because the expression "Great Wall of California"[56] has been used in describing them in a wider geographic context. As we have seen, the stone segments

---

[54] See "The Klamath Balance" and "The Modocs and a World's Heart."

[55] This term distinguishes these features from the linear "stone rows" of Europe that are comprised of separated stones, which should be compared instead with Native examples of closely positioned stones that align with landscape features; in these cases, however, the stones are not stacked, and so these are not cairns.

[56] E.g. Oscar Valverde and Raul Marquez, "The 'Great Wall' of California," *Ancient American*, volume 5, number 34, Colfax, WI, August/September 2000.

Linear cairns upon the landscape

Running straight or curving through the terrain, these constructions may be found clustered in specific areas inconsistent with modern development. The stones comprising them vary in size from the megalithic to others moveable by hand. The cairns vary considerably in length, with measurements in yards or in miles, and sometimes link to natural formations; rarely do the cairns exceed a few feet in height; and though they may intersect, or bifurcate, and form angles, they do not as a rule form any sort of enclosure. A single example might be accorded any number of mundane explanations, but each hypothesis would fail if a larger representative sample were considered. Above is an example of cairns in the Shasta River valley, and in the foreground they may be seen upon the steep face of a hill above former wetlands; such cairns cannot be dismissed as property lines, fences for animals, game drive lines, remnants from the clearing of fields, or as the result of child's play.

of the "China Wall" have never been associated with the Modocs, despite the fact that an example of a comparable structure was constructed by them in historic times, and that the stone wall formerly at the Link River was identified in Native lore as the creator Gmukamp's handiwork. For these reasons alone, we may presume that such cairns are essential rather than foreign to Native civilization, despite the American settlers' unwillingness to credit their enemies. Whereas the commonplace existence of small, non-linear "rock piles" was easily recognized by white settlers as expressions of Native belief,[57] the linear cairns must have presented certain inexplicable characteristics. The stone structures in the "China Wall," for example, are discontinuous, with deliberate gaps in their meandering course. Repurposing was necessary in order to give them a reason to exist in the minds of the settlers, and so the very existence of the cairns in the "China Wall" conveniently came to be attributed to this historic repurposing.[58]

Wider awareness of such cairns first appears in the newspapers of the San Francisco Bay Area soon after their mention in the Klamath Basin in 1885. In 1896, an article in the *San Francisco Chronicle* describes "ancient walls" in the Berkeley Hills and suggests a military purpose for them, while bemoaning the lack of "satisfactory" explanation as to their origin: "The survivors of the Mexican regime in California who are scattered on the ranches throughout the hills can give no information concerning the origin of the walls, which they say were there long before their fathers came to this

---

[57] William J. Clarke, op. cit.

[58] Repurposing projects may very well account for stories of crews, usually Chinese, put to work on walls elsewhere in California, especially since such accounts are not well documented. However, there are walls near Telegraph City that are considered the work of a Scottish stonemason, James Sykes; and there is no reason to doubt this, since the region is unusual in that its stone constructions often form ranching enclosures.

country. The Mexicans look on them with aversion and claim that the place is haunted by the ghost of a wicked old Don..."[59] In the early 1900s, Harold French wrote for more than a decade and more than one paper on what he argued was a genuine mystery. A *San Francisco Chronicle* headline from 1904 illustrates his perspective: "Who Built the Prehistoric Walls topping Berkeley Hills? Do the Miles of Mysterious Stone Barriers, Which Serve No Modern Purpose, Bespeak a Lost Civilization of Toltecs or Atlanteans?"[60] After French, reporting on what had become known as the "Berkeley Mystery Walls" was rare, until the 1980s, when interest was renewed due to the efforts of amateur researcher Russell Swanson. Swanson tried in vain to solicit the support of academics in his work, who cited a lack of funding, though he nevertheless contributed to a better popular understanding of the cairns. Swanson discovered that the stone network extended far south of the Berkeley Hills, and so the "Berkeley Mystery Walls" have become known as the "East Bay Walls," which is more appropriate, since only a single example seems to have survived development in the vicinity of Berkeley.

During the 20th century, the greatest authority on the mysteries of the East Bay was not writing for the newspapers, however. Sister Maria of Mission San Jose was born Countess Paula von Tessen in Denmark. Entering the Dominican Order in Europe, she was

---

[59] Volume LXIII, number 58, 8 March 1896.
[60] 14 August 1904. In an article for the *Oakland Tribune* in 1916 (magazine section of Sunday, October 15), he includes a sensible rebuttal to an academic's dismissive suggestion that the walls were sheep corrals or property markers; concerning the former, French cites the absence of enclosures. The cogency of his rebuttal is noteworthy, if only because the puerile suggestion persists.

transferred to San Francisco in 1907 and then to the Motherhouse at the foot of Mission Peak[61].

> She often hiked (mostly alone, but sometimes in the company of other nuns) over miles of hills and walls, in good weather and bad. They used probes, trowels, picks and wisk brooms in search of evidence. She was never seen without a textbook...Sister Mary Raymond at San Jose's Dominican Convent said of her, "In a way, she was a sort of genius and, perhaps, ahead of her time. She was thorough and methodical in her work."[62]

Her passing in 1959 allows for a half-century of research into the "East Bay Walls" and related discoveries, thoroughly recorded. The convent's physician, Robert B. Fisher, who shared an interest in the stone monuments, discovered that after her passing much of her research, including her "rock wall investigations," had been apparently destroyed to "'protect her senility.'" According to Dr. Fisher, Sister Mary Paula von Tessen was "a Sanskrit scholar whose notes and photographs and drawings for a book 'The Origin of Religion viewed from a prehistorical angle" was gently but firmly repressed by the Dominican Sisters..." As a consequence, we know precious little of Sister Maria's "interpretation of the walls and megaliths around the Mission Peak relating to those of the 'Old World.'"[63]

---

[61] Before electrical power was extended to Mission Peak, a phenomenon known as the Mission Peak Lights confounded locals. Lights are, of course, often associated with sacred peaks.
[62] Valverde and Marquez, page 34.
[63] Letter to Bill Sonin dated 16 August 1993, Bill Sonin Papers, Bancroft Library, University of California, Berkeley. Given the intellectual pursuits of the Dominican Order specifically, it is surely not Sister Mary's investigations in themselves that could

Authorities on the Native culture of the San Francisco Bay, such as Malcolm Margolin, are of little help, since it is supposed that the Ohlone people, who the Spanish encountered when they arrived, did not build with stone. Nevertheless, the Ohlone had succeeded other groups belonging to a more distant past, and the stones of San Francisco Bay still testify to the presence of others. In the North Bay, atop Ring Mountain on the Tiburon Peninsula, there are Pecked Curvilinear Nucleated petroglyphs (PCNs) attributed to Hokan or Penutian speaking peoples and dated to some 5000 to 8000 years before the present.[64] There is also a linear cairn on the same peninsula, a reminder at least that "East Bay Walls" is still an insufficient name. Even "Great Wall of California" is a misnomer, since it is not a single wall, although sensational claims of a 50-mile-long ridgetop barrier persist; and there is no doubt that other examples exist outside of California, for example in Washington, near the former Celilo Falls on the Columbia River in the vicinity of perhaps the oldest continually inhabited site in North America (that is, until 1957 and the building of the Dalles Dam).

If the range of these cairns is extended eastward,[65] well-known examples may also be found along the Continental Divide in Colorado, and these have been examined by professional archaeologists.

---

be blamed on "senility," but rather any thoughts out of keeping with Church doctrine.

[64] The Modoc language is considered Penutian.

[65] In 1939, it was estimated that some 250000 miles of stone walls cover the Eastern United States, and it would be paltry (to say the least) to deny the possibility that repurposing of pre-Colonial linear cairns was involved. In Southern Appalachia, academics have made progress in at least recognizing linear cairns as belonging to Native civilization (cf. Loubser and Frink, "An Archaeological and Ethnohistorical Appraisal of a Piled Stone Feature Complex in the Mountains of North Georgia," *Early Georgia*, volume 38, number 1).

Some Remarks on the "Mystery Walls"

Theorizing that the "walls" belong to "game drive" complexes, since no non-Native hypothesis is tenable, the archaeologists have confirmed that they are indeed precontact, and that the complexes may have been in use for some 10000 years.[66] Predictably, the theory is dictated by a materialistic perspective, according to which only a preoccupation with material subsistence could account for miles of stone constructions; and this modern belief passes over the inconvenience of their extreme elevation, and lacks supporting evidence and any clear notion of what was even hunted.[67] In this connection, it is worth quoting René Guénon regarding sciences such as archaeology:

> ...these sciences are characterized by the absence of any attachment to principles of a superior order, and thus the things taken as the objects of their study must themselves be thought of as being without any such attachment...if a contrary admission were made, science would at once be compelled to recognize that the real nature of its object eludes it.[68]

No doubt the complete refusal of archaeology to even admit the existence of the "Mystery Walls" in California is strange, and is itself an important indication of their

---

[66] Jason M. LaBelle and Spencer R. Pelton, "Communal hunting along the Continental Divide of Northern Colorado: Results from the Olson game drive (5BL147)," *Quaternary International*, May 2013.

[67] Instead, the supposed circular "hunting blinds" hollowed from the rocks could be compared with the "vision pits" near linear cairns in the Cascade Mountains of the Far West, or with the 19 unexplained pits upon Fort Mountain in Georgia.

[68] *The Reign of Quantity and the Signs of the Times*, Baltimore: Penguin Books, 1972, page 212.

real nature. Unlike the archaeologists, Guénon's exact contemporary Sister Maria Paula von Tessen, having dedicated herself to the superior principles of the religious life, was doubtless in the best position to illuminate the nature of the mysteries that demanded her attention, and so the loss of her "thorough and methodical" work is incalculable.

∇

Despite the suppression of Sister Maria's work, the purpose of the linear cairns may be divined from other indications. For example, there must surely be a correspondence between their function and the two locations in the West where they have by far the greatest concentration: first and foremost Mount Shasta, the Modoc Heart of the World, and secondly the Sutter Buttes in the Sacramento Valley. These peaks in fact represent the two principal centers of an eschatological landscape of traditional California, since according to the lore of many Native peoples, each mountain serves as a gathering place for the souls of the deceased.[69] Further, these peaks provide access to the posthumous states, usually involving traditional conceptions of the Milky Way. As I recently described in *Sacred Geography and the Paths of the Sun*, these conceptions are in perfect agreement with those of the Pythagoreans, and the doctrines of the latter provide the traditional context for

---

[69] On the Sutter or Marysville Buttes, see Roland B. Dixon, *The Northern Maidu*, New York: American Museum of Natural History, 1905, page 260; on Mount Shasta, see *Sacred Geography and the Paths of the Sun*, page 106, and cf. Powers (op. cit., page 260) on the Ghost Dance among the Shasta, who said "a crow had imparted to them the information that all their dead were hovering about the top of Mount Shasta, waiting a favorable moment to descend."

understanding recent discoveries relating to the sacred geography of Europe. Specifically, the azimuth of the summer solstice sunset may serve to indicate the principle pathway for souls upon the earth, and so it is of great interest to observe that the linear cairns in the vicinity of Mount Shasta are clustered exactly to the northwest of the mountain, that is, in the direction of the summer solstice sunset. That is not all: in my recent work I mentioned the solstitial relationship between landmarks on Tule Lake and Mount Shasta, and the knowledge specific to Gmukamp concerning the Paths of the Sun; in the direction of the summer solstice sunset from Tule Lake, however, there are places named "Sheepy" after the Native word Shapasheny, signifying the place where the Sun and Moon live, as well as the network of linear cairns near Hot Creek and the supposed "dams" formerly on the Link River.[70] Most remarkable of all, perhaps, is that the latter were traditionally attributed to Gmukamp, the "Old Man of the ancients," who knows the Paths of the Sun to the Land of the Dead.[71]

Perhaps the best-known literary visit to a land of the dead belongs to the sixth book of Virgil's *Aeneid*. Guided by the Cumaean Sybil, the hero visits the shades of the dead in the Underworld; but before doing so, he pauses at the gates of the temple of Apollo to examine the

---

[70] See "The Klamath Balance" and "The Modocs and a World's Heart," especially the former concerning the supernatural equilibrium traditionally present here at the headwaters of the Klamath River that was destroyed by the American invasion.

[71] Given the meaning of the name "Gmukamp," Flight-Lieutenant Maitland's seminal report from Arabia should not be overlooked, since the arrangements of linear cairns that he observed were identified by the Bedouin as the "works of the Old Men" (Maitland, "The 'Works of the Old Men' in Arabia," *Antiquity*, volume 1, issue 2, Cambridge University Press, June 1927). Curiously, however, the Arabian cairns most often form enclosures, and repeat various patterns that researches have named.

design of a labyrinth. Given its subject matter, the *Aeneid*'s sixth book is its most explicitly Pythagorean, since Pythagoras was above all recognized as an authority on the fate of the soul. In his study of the "Cumaean Gates," W. F. Jackson Knight attempts to explain the initiatory meaning of Virgil's book by including myths "from tribes of the Pacific islands and mainland coasts, and North America"[72] related to the journey of the soul after death. He quotes an account from Melanesia that is of particular interest:

> "Ghosts of the dead of the Seniang district pass along a 'road' to Wies, the land of the dead. At a certain point on their way they come to a rock...Always sitting by the rock is a female ghost Temes (i.e. 'ghost') Savsap, and on the ground in front of her is drawn the complete geometrical figure known as 'Nahal,' 'the Path'...As each ghost comes along the road, the guardian ghost hurriedly rubs out one half of the figure. The ghost now comes up, but loses his track and cannot find it...If he knows this figure, he at once completes the half which Temes Savsap rubbed out; and passes down the track through the middle of the figure. If, however, he does not know the figure, the Temes, seeing he will never find the road, eats him, and he never reaches the abode of the dead."[73]

---

[72] In *Vergil: Epic and Anthropology*, New York: Barnes & Noble, 1967, page 144.

[73] Ibid., pages 150-1. Cf. Arputharani Sengupta, *Buddhist Jewels in Mortuary Cult: Magic Symbols*, Agam, 2019, page xxxviii: "In the freehand Sona sand drawing of Angola the eternal knot in funerary rituals gives ceremonial safe passage to the departed. The Chokwe shaman at the end obliterates half of the interlaced

Some Remarks on the "Mystery Walls"

What is of particular interest here is the notion of an incomplete labyrinth pattern that confuses the ignorant soul. A "labyrinth" is literally a "place of stone."[74] If the landscape towards the summer solstice sunset from Mount Shasta is traditionally a place through which souls must pass, they would face there a vast but strangely incomplete labyrinth, a most bewildering pattern indeed.

This is not to say that every linear cairn is upon a path of the dead, even though we have seen stories of ghosts at both the "China Wall"[75] and "Mystery Walls," in locations far removed.[76] René Guénon, in considering the study by Jackson Knight, reminds us that the ritual value of the labyrinth was in the defense against "hostile psychic influences,"[77] and ghosts should no doubt be included among such influences. More generally, if these cairns appear to be concentrated in particular areas, this likely indicates the presence of unseen powers in the traditional understanding of these places. Evidence in support of this may be observed in the relationship we have already encountered between water and the linear cairns, or "dams." This relationship is in fact very often demonstrated by the placement of the cairns with respect to waterways and springs. Of course, Aeneas' passage required crossing the river of the Underworld, and Jackson Knight confirms the importance of water in the examples from the Pacific as well. In Native American cosmology, water is very specifically related to the realm of the Underworld. According to traditional lore both

---

endless maze right down the middle to block the spirit from retracing its way back to the land of the living."
[74] Ibid., page 149.
[75] See "The Modocs and a World's Heart."
[76] It is worth noting that in 1869, the first recorded opinion about the linear cairns near the Continental Divide thought them to be some sort of sepulcher.
[77] Cf. "The Cave and the Labyrinth," *Symbols of Sacred Science*, op. cit.

East and West[78], the horned serpents are denizens of this watery Underworld, and so it is worth recalling the use of a linear cairn for a "vision quest blind" by a Shawnee medicine man seeking such a serpent.[79] From evidence outside of North America, A. K. Coomaraswamy includes horned serpents among the guardians of the Sundoor, that is, the destination of the Path of the Sun.[80]

While it might be imagined that the *Aeneid* is an improbable place to find evidence relating to the "Mystery Walls," it would appear that this possibility was anticipated by Sister Maria Paula von Tessen herself. Given that the Cumaean Sibyl of the *Aeneid* was a servant of the Hyperborean Apollo[81] at his temple, and that Pythagoreanism is by definition Apollonian, it is very remarkable that in notes copied by Dr. Fisher, Sister Maria drew attention to the account of Diodorus of Sicily concerning the Hyperboreans and the temple of Apollo in Hyperborea. This reference to the Northern source of the Apollonian tradition is far from academic, since it is perhaps the best model we have for understanding the

---

[78] For a western example, see "The Great Horned Serpent" in P. E. Goddard, *Kato Texts*, Berkeley: The University Press, 1909, pages 226-7.
[79] Loubser and Frink, page 32. In the Eastern United States, there is a curious insistence upon viewing the cairns as serpent effigies; if accurate, this would suggest a local modification of the wider tradition, not in evidence in the West, serving an apotropaic purpose against a specific danger.
[80] *Guardians of the Sundoor: Late Iconographic Essays and Drawings of Ananda K. Coomaraswamy*, edited by Robert A. Strom, Louisville: Fons Vitae, 2004, pages 25-6, 50, 54.
[81] Since we are concerned here with cairns, it is worth recalling the name "Apollo Karneios" that Guénon considers in his article on "The Symbolism of Horns" (*Symbols of Sacred Science*, op. cit.) and that he relates to "cairn," as well as his unrealized hope "someday to return in a more complete way to the subject of the Hyperborean Apollo." Apollo, of course, is the slayer of the Underworld serpent Pytho, whence originates the name preserved by the "Pythagoreans."

intervention of the Primordial Tradition in prehistory that resulted in the birth of so many traditional forms. In *The Red and the White* I explored the evidence in North America for such a development.

As for the labyrinth, its ritual importance may be assumed to derive from this Hyperborean influence, since it is found in the context of so many traditional forms, including ones very far removed from the Classical world.[82] More significant still, the labyrinth's association in the Classical tradition with King Minos of Crete provides an indication of its true source. René Guénon explains in *The King of the World* that the name Minos is a title synonymous with the name of Manu, the "primordial legislator:" "This name moreover does not designate a more or less legendary historical personage, but rather a principle, a cosmic Intelligence that reflects pure spiritual light and formulates the Law (*Dharma*) appropriate to the conditions of our world and of our cycle of existence."[83] Regarding Minos in particular, Guénon adds a note of particular relevance here: "Among the Greeks, Minos was at the same time both legislator of the living and judge of the dead."[84] Here again, then, the symbolism of the labyrinth is inseparable from a principle having authority over the posthumous state of souls.

∇

---

[82] Jackson Knight's colleague John Layard presented a paper with the wonderful title, "The Labyrinth in the megalithic areas of Malekula, the Deccan, Scandinavia and Scotland."

[83] Op. cit., page 6. Recall the Native American association of Mount Shasta with the World's Heart, where the "Supreme Intelligence is vested."

[84] Ibid. As late as the Middle Ages, King Minos preserved his role as Judge of the Dead, as demonstrated by his inclusion in Dante's *Inferno*.

The near-complete ignorance of these linear cairns has, of course, failed to protect them against repurposing or removal, as was suggested above. In the early 20th century, the most well-known of the "Berkeley Mystery Walls" was an intersection of two cairns on the south slope of Round Top, yet of this structure nothing now remains. With the principle of "Chesterton's Fence" in mind,[85] according to which anything in place should not be removed without knowing its purpose, it is unsettling that the ancient cairns were demolished despite being located upon land set aside for its scientific interest; more disturbing still is a comparison with the Cretan Labyrinth, the purpose of which was to confuse the monstrous Minotaur.[86] Beyond this, it is very strange indeed that on the opposite site of Round Top, modern labyrinths have been rather mysteriously built within an abandoned quarry, and that the site is now popularly referred to as the "Volcanic Witch Project."

The developments upon Round Top are not the only example of caricature or mockery in these matters. Mount Shasta is above all associated in the popular imagination with the so-called "Lemurians," supposed survivors of an imaginary lost continent in the Pacific. What is rarely considered, however, is that the name "Lemurian" derives ultimately from Lemures, the hostile ghosts of ancient Rome. Not only does this concept derive from the same Classical milieu as the *Aeneid*, but Mount Shasta has become haunted, at least in the imagination, by the very forces the linear cairns may have served to guard against. As for the supposed builders of the cairns, the insistence on naming the Chinese has been noted, and this may either be illogically situated in the wake of the Gold Rush, or even in the nonsensical context of the Ming treasure fleet of Cheng Ho; but these presumptions only

---

[85] See "The Klamath Balance."
[86] Round Top in Sibley Volcanic Regional Preserve is one of two vents associated with an ancient volcano; the other, larger vent is now beneath the Berkeley Lab.

obscure the much more ancient and mysterious link between the Far East and Far West that is so worthy of consideration.[87] For example, it is very instructive indeed to compare these linear cairns with the so-called "spirit walls" of the Far East, since the latter are low barriers near gateways designed to bar harmful influences.

It is sufficient, of course, to recognize in these comparisons the imprints of the Primordial Tradition. It is hardly surprising, then, that very comparable examples of very ancient linear cairns might be pointed out worldwide. What seems to be especially unique about Native America is the number of surviving examples, many of which show no repurposing; after all, the conquering of America occurred only relatively recently, especially in the West, and an "age of stone" was long preserved here free of the developments occurring elsewhere. Even so, amateur speculations all too often insist on divorcing the cairns from Native life, echoing the beliefs of early Americans that Native peoples were preceded by a superior civilization from elsewhere, usually of giants.[88] The availability of satellite imagery has certainly offered amateur investigators ample mysterious evidence, but if their staggering number is any indication, the cairns bespeak a very long presence on this land for those responsible.[89] Given the apparent

---

[87] See *The Red and the White* and "The Modocs and a World's Heart." Another relevant example might be to compare Chinese "Lao," a name suggesting "undying," with Llao, the Klamath name for a mythological figure of the Underworld.

[88] The absence of this imaginary civilization in turn justified the "Indian removal," with Indians deserving the same treatment that they must have inflicted upon their supposed predecessors. On the matter of giants, cf. *The Red and the White*, pages 19-21; why they should be the builders of low cairns is never considered.

[89] Obviously we have seen in the case of the San Francisco Bay a succession of Native groups, but in the example of the Modocs, "archaeologists believe that they have remained here from at least 12,000 years ago" (John Allison, "The Cultural Landscape

purpose of the cairns, however, the technological unveiling of their ubiquity is no doubt a sign of the times, as well as of the import of the American landscape. Native silence regarding them is to be expected; the linear cairns concern the Unseen and the ultimate fate of their people, and Americans have never shown much regard for either.[90]

---

of the Klamath, Modoc and Yahooskin Peoples: Spirit, Nature, History, Part Two," National Park Service, 1995). Even with a succession of groups, it is likely that later peoples had a hand in extending the cairns, or at least in preserving them.

[90] Even when academics have recognized the importance of eschatology in Native tradition, they have displayed an embarrassing degree of condescension, using terminology like "Southern Death Cult."

Linear cairn in the Klamath River canyon
Here a low wall separates burials from a village that had been occupied for at least 7000 years.

Simloki's shadow upon the Fall River Valley

∇

Racing Shadows

Given the destruction of traditional America that resulted from the immigration of Europeans, it is not too surprising that we often lack traditional perspectives on its sacred landscapes. This is true especially in the West, where genocidal policies were pursued with particular ferocity, although wherever Native peoples were relocated from their lands, the knowledge of those landscapes was likewise removed. Fortunately, there are exceptions, such as the knowledge that has been preserved among a people that still live in their ancestral lands along the Pit River of California. Nine of the eleven bands of the Pit River Indians are properly known as the Achumawi, and one of their leaders, Floyd Buckskin, has in recent years provided valuable information on their sacred landscape. Working alongside modern academics, in particular the archaeologist Arlene Benson, Buckskin has made generous contributions to our understanding, even sharing, for example, his insights on the correspondences between celestial events and the landscape.[91]

---

[91] See for example Benson and Buckskin, "How the Seasons Began: An Ajumawi Narrative Involving Sun, Moon, North Star, and South Star," *Griffith Observer*, volume 51 number 7, Los Angeles: Griffith Observatory, July 1987.

In a collection of academic papers Benson helped prepare,[92] Floyd Buckskin is listed as the co-author with Jack M. Broughton of "Racing Simloki's Shadow: The Ajumawi Interconnection of Power, Shadow, Equinox, and Solstice." Buckskin is the source here of traditional lore concerning a sacred mountain near the Fall River Valley of his people's domain, and specifically concerning the shadow cast by this Simloki or Soldier Mountain. As the sun sets, the mountain's shadow moves upon the valley as a balanced triangle. That is not all: according to Buckskin, on the occasion of the quarter days of the solar year, this shadow points to the distant locations of several sacred springs in turn as it shifts in accordance with the Sun's position.[93] Even more remarkably, perhaps, is that people in former times participated in this phenomenon by racing Simloki's shadow across the valley. Buckskin further specifies this mountain as a "men's power place." In confirmation of the peak's sanctity, there have been cupules found upon a boulder at its summit, where a modern fire lookout has replaced whatever more transient markers might have formerly existed there. According to Benson and Buckskin, "cupules at certain places are said to be the footprints left by the First People, which imbue the rocks with power," and that such places are "where power is concentrated and for this reason are visited by people

---

[92] *Earth and Sky: Papers from the Northridge Conference on Archaeoastronomy*, edited by Benson and Hoskinson, Thousand Oaks: Slo'w Press, 1985.
[93] See ibid. for a graphic depiction of the "dynamics of Simloki's shadow." Despite the authors' representation of solstitial alignments, the sacred springs are not necessarily positioned upon solstitial alignments from the mountain, since the afternoon shadow must turn somewhat as the sun arcs towards its azimuth; the shadow at the equinoxes, however, would proceed in a straighter course towards the distant edge of the valley where the springs are located.

who wish to acquire power."[94] In other words, Simloki would also have been a place to visit, even if the race against its shadow involved running away from the mountain.

These valuable recollections of a people's sacred landscape invite a number of remarkable comparisons to be made with other expressions of tradition. To begin with, the best-known example of a mountain's triangular shadow being cast upon a landscape belongs to a sacred peak in Sri Lanka, formerly Ceylon, where Buddhist pilgrims especially gather to witness the sunrise event; but as the Buddhist name of the mountain, Sri Pada, indicates, it is not the mountain's shadow that attracts pilgrims. "Pada" means "foot," since there is upon the summit of the sacred mountain a footprint in stone that is venerated as that of the historical Buddha. For Christians and Muslims, however, who likewise undertake pilgrimages to the mountain they call Adam's Peak, the miraculous footprint belongs to Adam, the "first man." Clearly it is this attribution that accords so closely with the Achomawi teaching on the footprints of the "First People." Of course, for the Islamic tradition, it is not only Adam, with whom prophecy originated, who is believed to have left footprints in stone. As I have explained elsewhere,[95] the place for prayer at the Holy Ka`ba in Mecca is marked by a footprint of Abraham, who is the "Pole" of prophecy. Above all, however, it is the "Seal" of prophecy, the Last Prophet Muhammad, whose footprints are venerated throughout the Muslim world, since it is believed that while his footstep left no trace upon sand, its imprint would be left upon stone.

Included in the traditional accounts of his holy life is a story that is unmistakably reminiscent of our Achumawi subject. The setting of this story, the mountain

---

[94] "Achomawi Jumping Rocks and the Concept of the Test," *American Indian Rock Art Papers*, volume 15, 1992.
[95] Cf. *The Red and the White* and *Sacred Geography and the Paths of the Sun* on the matter of footprints in stone.

of Uhud, is a sacred mountain in Islam, with its own spiritual identity, just as for the Achumawi, Simloki is no less than a "sacred entity" and "spirit-being."[96]

> Once the Prophet called his Companions when the sun was rising and told them to run towards a mountain (Jabal Uhud) with the sun at their backs and catch their shadows. Whoever caught their shadow would be rewarded with the Prophet's robe...As they ran with the sun at their backs, their shadows were running away from them...When they reached the mountain he told them to turn around and, "Run towards me." Then the shadows were running behind after them as they ran to the Prophet. He said, "O my Companions, whoever is running after this worldly life is like one running after his shadow, and he will never get it. Whoever is running towards ākhira (towards me and the message that I brought from Allāh) this world will run after him like your shadow was running after you."[97]

Taken together, the shared elements of sacred mountain, shadow, and footrace all invite a comparison to be made between these two traditional accounts. However, it is clear that the race of the Holy Prophet's Companions was towards the sacred mountain and not away; but with the Sun behind the racers in both cases, we can imagine that the racers of Simloki's shadow would at the same time have been "chasing" their own. Now, by successfully

---

[96] Broughton and Buckskin, op. cit.
[97] Shaykh Muhammad Hisham Kabbani, *The Approach of Armageddon? An Islamic Perspective*, Fenton: ISCA, 2003, page 225.

outrunning Simloki's shadow (an incomprehensible feat by any stretch of the imagination), it was believed that worldly benefits would be acquired: "good luck in hunting, leadership, and reproduction;" and in the same article a successful racer in historic times is singled out for being especially long-lived. In the example of the Companions of the Prophet Muhammad, such concerns are symbolized by their shadows, and so are explicitly opposite the orientation towards the Prophet and, of course, the Sun. In Islamic terms, this world is *dunya* and its complement is *ākhira*; the latter literally refers to the next world after *dunya*, or the Afterlife.

    Obviously there is no change of direction in the Achumawi race, but a detail passed over by Broughton and Buckskin must be given fuller treatment if we are to better understand this sacred landscape, and so do justice to our subject. The authors note the proximity of Mount Shasta to the northwest of Simloki, but they do not mention that this spiritual center of the Native cosmos[98] is in fact aligned with the azimuth of the summer solstice sunset from the much smaller sacred height. Their reticence is curious, to say the least, since knowledge of the Sun's position on the quarter days is fundamental to their paper. I had occasion to mention this azimuth through Achumawi lands in my study of solar alignments, *Sacred Geography and the Paths of the Sun*. These alignments are related to the Pythagorean doctrine of the solstices as gateways for souls entering and exiting this world. Along with the Pythagoreans, the Achumawi regard the Milky Way as a "pathway of spirits," and the astronomer E.C. Krupp relates that this pathway is reached from Mount Shasta at the time of the summer solstice: "the Ajumawi say the Milky Way is aligned at this time with the trail followed on the Earth by the dead

---

[98] Cf. "The Modocs and a World's Heart."

and aligned with the Sun as well."[99] Not surprisingly, the source of the doctrine related by Krupp is none other than Floyd Buckskin, and so Buckskin not only knew Mount Shasta as a place for souls to depart this world, but also that Simloki was aligned with it. Nevertheless, these considerations were not considered relevant, apparently, to the racing of Simloki's shadow in this world.[100]

The inclusion of Mount Shasta into our view of Simloki introduces a new dimension related not to this world but to the next. From the summit of Simloki, where "footprints" of the First People had been found, there are then two orientations to be considered: away from the Sun in search of worldly gain, or towards it when its azimuth on the summer solstice[101] marks a time for reaching the Afterlife. From this perspective, the comparison with the story of the Prophet and his Companions is clearly complete. There is at first a movement outward from the "spirit-being," and this is reenacted in the racing of shadows, whether from the presence of the Prophet or from the sunlight upon Simloki.[102] Afterwards, there must be a return, and this is made explicit in the example from Islam, but it is likewise

---

[99] E.C. Krupp, "Negotiating the Highwire of Heaven: The Milky Way and the Itinerary of the Soul," *Vistas in Astronomy*, volume 39, issue 4, 1995.

[100] It is worth noting that Buckskin does not describe the trail of the soul upon the Earth as straight, but as wandering down the Pit River before returning to Mount Shasta. This may represent a reconciliation between the axial function of Mount Shasta and the Native view of the Land of the Dead as downriver. From the valley, of course, it is to the West that the waters of the river, so essential for life, ultimately flow.

[101] If the solstitial alignment is extended beyond Simloki to the southeast, its course reaches a zone near the Pit River that is marked by linear cairns similar to those northwest of Mount Shasta. Cf. "Some Remarks on the Mystery Walls."

[102] On spiritual authority and the symbolism of mountains, including among the Achumawi, see *The Red and the White*, page 50.

possible for the Achumawi, since a "path of the sun" leads on the "gateway" of the summer solstice to the earthly embodiment of the Heart of the World, Mount Shasta, from whence the celestial world is reached. It should be observed that in both examples, the movement away from the sacred is not an expression of rebellion against it, but is rather directed by it. Obviously we are dealing here with a cosmogonic process, of an expansion of possibilities that must be followed by a return to a transcendent principle. In all this the symbolism of the heart is most appropriate, since it is the heart with its rhythm that governs the circulation of life within the channels of the human microcosm. These examples unite the Islamic and Achumawi traditions in example as well as in principle: "in the Islamic tradition the sphere of pure primordial light is the *Rūh muhammadiyyah*, which is also the 'Heart of the World;' and the entire 'cosmos' is vivified by the 'pulsations' of this sphere."[103]

It is significant that Broughton and Buckskin are by no means sure as to the timing of the race against Simloki's shadow; all they can say is that the event appears related to the quarter days, that is, the very days that express through the Sun's position the full range of temporal possibilities.[104] The shadow of the mountain rotates, as it were, throughout the year upon the world of the valley below. This moving shadow was believed to present a real danger for the racers: "…when racing the shadow you are actually racing a spirit-being. And if you should look back, while racing, to see how you are doing, the spirit-being would probably kill you on the spot."[105] Mythologically, this rotating mountain shadow therefore recalls the "turning castle" motif, concerning which we

---

[103] René Guénon, "The Heart and the World Egg," op. cit.
[104] The likeliest time for the race would surely be at the equinoxes, both because the weather would be most suitable and the course to the distant hills would be most direct and therefore shortest.
[105] Broughton and Buckskin, op. cit.

must turn to the insights of René Guénon's colleague Ananda Coomaraswamy: "'The turning castle has also its significance with respect to the Other World.' This Otherworld is at once a Paradise and the World of the Dead, and in post-Christian folklore to be identified with Fairyland; it may be located overseas to the West, or Under-wave, or in the Sky, but is always in various ways protected from all but the destined Hero who achieves the Quest."[106] Since it is "never to be found after sunset," as Coomaraswamy reminds us, the entrance to the Otherworld or next world is the Sundoor, and here the "sacred entity" Simloki is its guardian. Perhaps only those who outpaced its shadow were permitted to climb the mountain to the footprints of the First People at its summit. In keeping with the summer solstice as gateway or door, the solstice Sun leads from the summit of Simloki to the Heart of the World where this world is joined to the next.[107]

The traditions that formerly vivified the American sacred landscape have been tragically interrupted, but we are fortunate even to be reminded of them and to recognize in them the traces of the Primordial Tradition. The shadow of Simloki still moves across the land, and no matter the historical conditions of this world, it is to the next world that all souls must ultimately return.

---

[106] Ananda K. Coomaraswamy, "Symplegades," *Studies in Comparative Religion*, volume 7 number 1, Bedfont, 1973.

[107] In the example from the Islamic tradition, the setting of Uhud is better remembered as the location of the Battle of Uhud, when the Companions of the Prophet were honored to serve as guardians of the Prophet and so of the Heart of the World; and during this battle, reportedly, the mountain itself defended the Prophet against his enemies (cf. Hajjah Amina Adil, *Muhammad: the Messenger of Islam*, Fenton: ISCA, 2002, page 343).

Roman-styled water temple (above) juxtaposed with an ancient cupped stone in California (below)

EUROPE

∇

Idris in Wales

In considering the matter of the Seven Spiritual Centers of Britain,[108] another related mystery presents itself, namely the memory in the sacred geography of Wales of a prophet of Islam named Idris. Islam must indeed be specified here, and no doubt pause should be taken to consider the reason, that although the antediluvian prophet is known in the other Abrahamic traditions, he is only called by another name, Enoch. Only in Arabic – and apparently in Welsh – is this figure called Idris. There can be no question of a fortuitous coincidence here, since there is no detail of the Welsh memory that is out of keeping with Islamic tradition. He is characterized as a giant, for example, while Islamic lore insists on the gigantic stature of primordial humanity; and the knowledge attributed to him relates especially to the stars, while astrology in Islam is included among the sciences traced back to Idris. A coincidence might instead be recognized in the recent appearance of books relating to Idris in Wales, beginning with my work involving the Seven Centers, *Sacred Geography and the Paths of the Sun*. Two other works concerning the legacy of Idris in Wales to a greater or lesser extent have since appeared in quick succession: *The Giants of Stonehenge and Ancient Britain* by

---

[108] See *Sacred Geography and the Paths of the Sun*, pages 95 ff.

Hugh Newman and Jim Vieira, and *The Origin of the Zodiac: Cadair Idris and the Star Maps of Gwynedd* by Hugh Evans. Regarding this subject, then, attention is growing, and so there is more of a need to clarify some of its aspects.

It will be observed that the very titles of these two books refer precisely to the shared characteristics of Idris indicated above. Unfortunately, however, neither work shows any regard for Islam, despite the living character of this tradition in contrast to the Celtic tradition that has been lost.[109] In any event, the authors of *The Giants of Stonehenge and Ancient Britain* are nevertheless aware of Idris in Islam, for how else could they casually offer, in parentheses no less, that "Enoch was also known as Idris"?[110] Despite the authors' disregard for the source of this identification, it nonetheless provides them with the substance of their conclusion, that the geomancy apparent in the British landscape is evidence of "Enochian traditions in Britain." The authors then rely on the apocryphal Book of Enoch for their interpretations, and as a predictable consequence, they perpetuate contemporary confusions that fail to make any useful distinction between angels and the unholy giants or Nephilim, and even invoke the Mesopotamian Annunaki in accordance with New Age beliefs.

I have explained in *The Red and the White* that only by referencing Islamic doctrine may the nature of the "fallen angels" and Nephilim be properly understood. Again, according to Islamic cosmology, there are three classes of created beings to be considered here, and these classes correspond to the spiritual, psychic, and physical degrees. Angels correspond to the spiritual degree, while human beings occupy the physical world of bodies; the

---

[109] It may be allowed that a reconstitution of Druidism has been attempted, but unfortunately by depriving it of the very support that might have allowed for its historical survival, Celtic Christianity.
[110] Glastonbury: Avalon Rising, 2021.

psychic degree is between them and is represented by the *jinn* or djinn. Just as the microcosmic psyche might be considered "angelic" if illuminated by spiritual discipline, the conflation of jinn with angels is rooted in the most ancient of times, when, according to traditional accounts, jinn reportedly kept company with the angels. Accounts of the "fall" from this holy company are familiar enough, yet a proper understanding of the Book of Enoch, and indeed of the Book of Genesis that refers to the fallen Watchers and Nephilim, demands recognizing the role of the jinn that consequently allows for the infallibility of the angels. This is not simply a matter of doctrine, however. René Guénon makes an important observation in *The Reign of Quantity and the Signs of the Times*: "The VIth chapter of Genesis might perhaps provide, in a symbolical form, some indications relating to the distant origins of the 'counter-initiation.'"[111] It is not at all surprising that a lack of clarity on this matter should be a hallmark of contemporary confusions, since the signs of the times all indicate the pervasiveness of the counter-initiation and its "inverted spirituality," to use Guénon's expression, even though the psychic here excludes the truly spiritual.

The failure of the authors of *The Giants of Stonehenge and Ancient Britain* to make recourse to Islamic doctrine is especially disappointing, given that Hugh Newman presents himself as a continuator of the work of John Michell.[112] As I have noted elsewhere,[113] Michell deferred to the authority of René Guénon, or Shaykh `Abdul-Wahid Yahya, on matters of symbolism; and in

---

[111] Op. cit., page 358.

[112] The conference that he organizes at Glastonbury is named "Megalithomania," after the book title by John Michell, and in 2021 gave the John Michell Memorial Lecture on Michell himself. Conference lectures are made available on Newman's Megalithomania video channel, and it is worth noting that the channel's theme music is a track entitled "Djinn."

[113] *Sacred Geography and the Paths of the Sun*, page 88.

his most popular book, Michell named Idris in the context of Islam.[114] It is of further interest to observe that Michell did not identify Idris with Enoch, but rather with Hermes, the divine messenger or intermediary of the Classical tradition; indeed, both identifications are to be found in Islam, with the latter deriving from Abu Ma`shar al-Balkhi's explanation of Hermes' epithet "Thrice-Great."[115] A number of useful indications are provided by Abu Ma`shar's explanation. For instance, by identifying the first Hermes as the antediluvian prophet Idris, the Hermetic sciences, which by their very nature are "intermediary" and relate to the psychic domain, are thereby attached to the spiritual light of prophecy. For Abu Ma`shar, the name "Hermes" is in fact a title, and so it is strange indeed that Newman and Vieira would offer that "Enoch may have been more of a title than a name;"[116] this suggestion mimics Islamic doctrine even while obscuring it.

As for the authors' references to Mesopotamia, they really become relevant only through an awareness of the postdiluvian Second Hermes who is specifically associated with the Chaldean tradition. Moreover, the Celtic and Chaldean traditions are in fact united through the person of Pythagoras. Abu Ma`shar names him as the student of the Second Hermes, and the Classical tradition relates that Pythagoras studied astronomy among the Chaldeans; and, as I have addressed, Pythagoreanism has long been linked to the Druids.[117] Amidst their wealth of material, Newman and Vieira refer to Pythagorean geometry in the context of Idris' legacy, but fail to appreciate just how relevant this material is. According to

---

[114] *The New View Over Atlantis*, San Francisco: Harper & Row, 1983, page 165.
[115] Cf. *Sacred Geography and the Paths of the Sun*, page 83. I offer another interpretation in *Alchemy in Middle-earth*, in order to facilitate a more spiritual than historical understanding.
[116] Op. cit., page 365.
[117] See *Sacred Geography and the Paths of the Sun*, pages 82 ff.

Diodorus of Sicily, the Druids followed the teaching of Pythagoras especially regarding the fate of the soul, and there is reason to accept that this doctrine persisted in Celtic Christianity. We have devoted an entire book to the Pythagorean "paths of the Sun" that align to the solstices and concern this doctrine; and so it is of particular interest that in northern Wales there are still churches that are likewise oriented to the solstices.[118] Northern Wales is precisely where the memory of Idris has been retained.

∇

The legacy of Idris in Wales is the particular focus of the book *The Origins of the Zodiac: Cadair Idris and the Star Maps of Gwynedd*, in which author Hugh Evans seeks to show a link between the landscape of northern Wales and the formulation of Ptolemaic astronomy. From the foregoing, it is clear that through the Thrice-Great Hermes, Islamic doctrine provides the link between Idris and the astronomy of Mesopotamia that is generally regarded as the source of the zodiac. While Evans concedes that "peoples of the Middle East know Hermes as Idris,"[119] he turns, like Hugh Newman who is in fact his colleague, to the Book of Enoch rather than Islamic Hermeticism. Leaving aside the author's dependence upon his own imagination to identify not only a zodiac but as many modern constellations as would fit upon his maps, there is no reason to reject his basic notion of a terrestrial correspondence with the stars that could be

---

[118] See Bernadette Brady, "The Dual Alignments of the Solstitial Churches in North Wales," *Journal of Skyscape Archaeology*, volume 3 number 1, 2017. The connection between these alignments and the Pythagorean tradition is not addressed.
[119] Digital location 375.

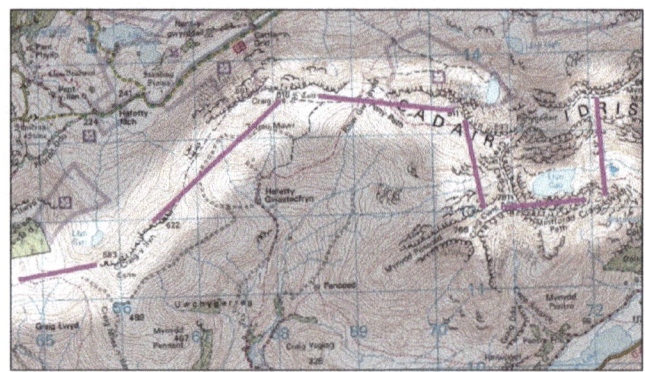

The topography of Cader Idris
Lines and highlighting by Hugh Evans

attributed to Idris in Wales. However, Evans actually seems to have taken his inspiration from another author, Mike Harris, who had already made a rough comparison between the asterism of the Big Dipper from the Ursa Major constellation and the topography of the mountain named as the "seat" (*cadair*) of Idris.

Now, Cadair or Cader Idris was included in my inventory of the Seven Spiritual Centers of Britain, and it will be recalled that the arrangement of these seven centers upon the British landmass was similarly compared to the heptagonal asterism. The duplication of this familiar pattern might be considered as yet another coincidence, but heptagonal arrangements have also been discerned in the topography of other centers. The hills at Glastonbury, for example, have likewise been seen as a representation of the Great Bear;[120] and the Seven Hills of Edinburgh, though they have not been accorded a stellar interpretation, nonetheless conform to a seven-fold

---

[120] Cf. John Michell, *New Light on the Ancient Mystery of Glastonbury*, Glastonbury: Gothic Image, 1990.

pattern. That is not all: the prototype of a landscape zodiac such as Evans claims to have discovered belongs to the Glastonbury environs, and we are fortunate indeed to have Guénon's observations concerning it.[121] Following the discovery of the Glastonbury Zodiac, British imaginations claimed to discover a great many more, and leaving aside questions of authenticity for these others, it is worth observing that zodiacs have been discerned in the landscapes of most of the Seven Spiritual Centers, including Edinburgh and the Pendle Hill region near Nelson, besides Glastonbury and now Cader Idris. Such a recurrence of characteristic elements serves as a reminder that spiritual "centers" are but projections of the supreme center. As far as the zodiac is concerned, it is important to recognize that its signs are positioned along the ecliptic in the sky, and that the ecliptic is the pathway for the wanderings of the planets, and that it is the planets that are assimilated to the highest ranks of the spiritual hierarchy. According to Islamic esoterism, Idris is the chief of that hierarchy and associated with the Sun, but his station is specifically called the "Pole" (*qutb*),[122] like the unmoving Pole Star alongside Ursa Major.

If Cader Idris serves as a "seat" for the Pole, it is perhaps natural to identify such a place as the supreme center. Such a confusion arises, in René Guénon's words, from "assimilating the image with the original center itself."[123] Unlike John Michell, none of the contemporary

---

[121] "The Land of the Sun," *Symbols of Sacred Science*.

[122] Guénon's characterization of the initiatory triangle as a "signature of the Pole" (see *Sacred Geography and the Paths of the Sun*, page 45) is the key to understanding the relevance of the "Triangle of Idris" mentioned by Newman and Vieira (op. cit., pages 332-3); in a most explicit example of confusion, however, the standing stone of Llech Idris is clearly shown in the wrong position on page 333.

[123] Ibid. Many of the claims of British Israelism concerning Biblical locations in Britain may be understood as confusions of this kind. Cf. *Sacred Geography and the Paths of the Sun*, page 97.

authors mentioned here give any attention to Guénon's teachings on spiritual centers and the corresponding spiritual hierarchy, and this is surely not unrelated to their failing to avail themselves of the living tradition of Islam. Unsurprisingly, examples of the aforementioned confusion are obvious in their works, such as Newman and Vieira's assimilation of Britain with Hyperborea, when Hyperborea is properly synonymous with the original center. Evans' strange insistence that the Ptolemaic constellations derive from the form of the Welsh landscape is no doubt due to a similar error. There is also his obsession with interpreting any word of significance, no matter its etymology, in terms of his Welsh language, but this again suggests a confusion between an image and its primordial source; in this case, the source is the so-called Syrian (*suryani*) language that Guénon mentions in the course of his study of the Glastonbury Zodiac.[124]

∇

A spiritual center is obviously associated with spirituality, but for spirituality to be present in a terrestrial or physical place, the intermediary psychic dimension must also be present. The psychic confusions of the New Age movement have long been well represented in Glastonbury, for example, and there remains a haunting reminder of this dimension in the Pendle Hill area near Nelson through its historical ties to

---

[124] Ibid. This "Adamic" language was sought in vain by the Elizabethan magus Dr. John Dee, who was himself involved in rather dubious "Enochian traditions in Britain." Even so, the Welshman Dr. Dee never mistook the Welsh language for that of Adam.

witchcraft.[125] As for Cader Idris, Newman and Vieira point out that "occult students still conduct their rituals on this spot, sensing the power that emanates from the mountain."[126] However, traditional lore insists that madness might result from spending a night upon the mountain's summit. Significantly, the Arabic word for a madman, *majnun*, derives from the same word as jinn.

In the context of the psychic power attached to a spiritual center, it is worth recalling Guénon's characterization of "psychic 'entities'" as guardians "which it is extremely dangerous for anyone to approach who has not got the required 'qualifications' and does not take the necessary precautions."[127] Guénon includes giants among such entities,[128] and so it is worth extending this interpretation to the scriptural accounts of the giants who prevented the Israelites from entering the Promised Land.[129] The story is especially pertinent here, because the one to first approach the giants and ultimately to vanquish them was the prophet Joshua, who in Islamic sacred geography becomes the guardian of Ottoman Constantinople; and because of the size of his tomb there,

---

[125] This haunted area became the setting for a series of young adult novels by Joseph Delaney, beginning with "The Spook's Apprentice."
[126] Op. cit., page 180.
[127] Guénon 1972, page 188. The author adds a description of how "forces of nature" are necessarily attached to these guardians, and this accounts for the role of giants as "sowers of thunder." Newman and Vieira provide many fascinating accounts of this theme, including from America.
[128] Giants are in a sense given physical form in the terrestrial zodiacs through the strange effigies that are seen to inhabit the courses of the landscape. It is likely that the imaginative perception of them relates to psychic impressions experienced by certain observers; for this reason, perhaps, while the landscape may accommodate the effigies because of the special character of the site, the physical evidence will always remain unconvincing to materialistic science.
[129] Cf. *Qur'an* V, 20-6.

Joshua is himself remembered as a giant.[130] According to this interpretation, then, the spiritual light of prophecy sanctifies the psychic domain, and this is embodied in the "spiritualized" giants who sanctify lands at the far ends of Europe. Yet these examples are surely exceptional; in any case what matters most is not the psychic aspect - and so not the lore of giants - but rather the spiritual power that chooses a particular place as a "seat."

The mystery remains how the name "Idris" came to be preferred to the name "Enoch" in the Christian land of Wales. It is even worth emphasizing that the Islamic name has been preferred to the Greek name "Hermes;" after all, through the doctrines of Pythagoras, it was to the Second Hermes rather than the first that the Celtic tradition seems to have been more closely related. However, just as binding the Hermetic sciences to Idris brings them into the light of prophecy, the same must be understood for the ancient sites in Wales that have been named for him. In the lands of Islam, the attachment of holy persons to ancient sites may be well known, but it should be insisted that sacred places associated with Idris are by no means common. Newman and Vieira draw attention to Tell Idris near Harran, where the ancient sanctity of Idris has been invoked in the context of an ancient mound.[131] A most extraordinary example of a site dedicated to him is the Great Pyramid of Egypt, the

---

[130] On the giant Joshua and Constantinople, cf. *Mysteries of Dune*, pages 38-9. On Joshua in all his aspects, see the eagerly anticipated volume by Karima Sperling.

[131] Op. cit., page 365. Before the excavation of Göbekli Tepe, the ancient mound had been the focus of an Islamic pilgrimage, apparently, doubtless due to a spiritual presence in the cemetery that had formerly dominated the site. It is moreover at least worth noting that in the iconography of Wales' patron saint, the namesake of the giant slayer David, the saint stands upon a mound that had moved, thereby indicating the saint's authority over the physical and psychic degrees. On the stabilizing function of saints, cf. *The Red and the White*, chapter 5.

supposed "tomb of Hermes;" but since no tomb could belong to Idris who is believed like Enoch to be ever-living, the Great Pyramid is best understood as a monument to his sciences.[132] No doubt the open attestation of Idris' Islamic authority in Wales is part of the special disclosure of the Seven Spiritual Centers of Britain.

The role of Idris is everywhere and always of supreme importance, since he is for the Primordial Tradition as he is for Islam the antediluvian embodiment and perennial holder of supreme spiritual authority. According to Islamic esoterism, many sciences are attributed to him: "alchemy (which "heals metals" and leads them back to the state of their original perfection by transforming them into gold), medicine, astrology, the knowledge of the laws of cosmology (`ilm al-`âlam);"[133] according to the same source, he is designated as the "Healer of Wounds" (Mudâwî l-Kulûm).[134] It has become critically clear that now more than ever, humanity's relationship with the sacred is in need of healing. In Wales, seemingly, there are places where the spirituality of this ever-living healer might still be sought. At the very least, the presence of Idris in Wales offers tangible support for the assertion of Guénon's inheritor, Michel Vâlsan, that "the Qutb provides his providential help not only to Muslims…"[135]

---

[132] Cf. René Guénon, "Hermes' Tomb," *Traditional Forms and Cosmic Cycles*, Hillsdale: Sophia Perennis, 2003.

[133] The principles of sacred geography are probably best classified under the "laws of cosmology (`ilm al-`âlam);" the term "geomancy" to which Newman and Vieira refer originates as the translation of the Arabic "divination by sand" (`ilm al-raml).

[134] He is so named in the *Futuhat al-Makkiyah* of Shaykh Muhyiddin Ibn `Arabi; the quotation is from Michel Chodkiewicz' introduction to Ibn al-`Arabi, *The Meccan Revelations*, volume II, New York, Pir Press, 2004, pages 35-6.

[135] "Les derniers hautes grades de l'Écossisme et la réalisation descendante," *Études Traditionnelles*, Paris, 1953.

Guardians of the Heart

∇

The Labyrinth of the Age of Gold

With its publication in 1966, *Les Mystères de la Cathédrale de Chartres* played no small part in popularizing some of the more arcane topics relating to Medieval European civilization. Of particular note is the attention given to the pre-Christian importance of Chartres that involved an emphasis on earth "energies," as well as the insistence upon the cathedral's sacred geometry. In this regard the author of the book, the journalist Louis Charpentier, anticipates the concerns of John Michell, whose seminal *The View Over Atlantis* was published in 1969. Charpentier singles out the role of the Knights Templar in these matters, and he moreover seems to have introduced the problematic notion that the Order was in possession of the Ark of the Covenant. By so doing, Charpentier may have hoped to help foster an understanding of the esoteric function of the Templars, who served for the Medieval West as "Guardians of the Holy Land;"[136] but it is worth recognizing that the proper understanding of this function has only become more and

---

[136] See the article with this title by René Guénon (*Symbols of Sacred Science*, op. cit.).

more grossly obscured by fantasies of lost treasure in the wake of Charpentier's work.[137]

Another of the author's musings that has been casually repeated concerns the specific placement of Gothic cathedrals, beginning with Chartres, upon the landscape of France. Dedicated like Chartres to "Our Lady" (*Notre Dame*) the Virgin Mary, these cathedrals seem to mirror the positions of the principal stars of the constellation Virgo, the Virgin (below).[138]

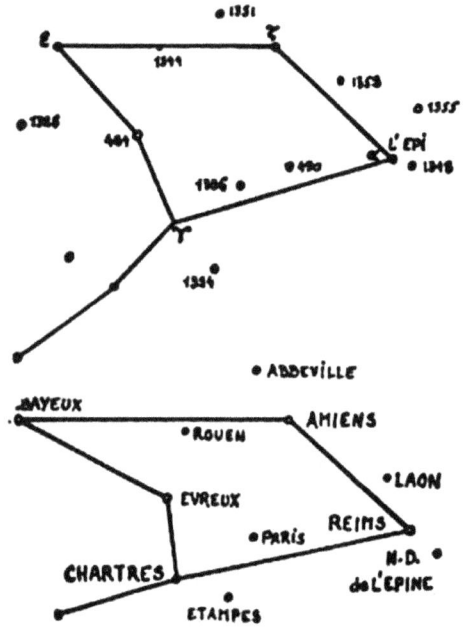

---

[137] A subsequent popular account of the Templars and the Ark, *The Sign and the Seal*, launched the career of journalist Graham Hancock in the field of "alternative" history (and prehistory).
[138] Louis Charpentier, *Les Mystères de la Cathédrale de Chartres*, Paris: Laffont, 1966, page 30.

The Labyrinth of the Age of Gold

Les Mystères de la Cathédrale de Chartres begins with the author observing a more tangible accommodation of celestial light within the cathedral's design. On the summer solstice, a ray of light illuminates a special stone upon the floor of the church, and the author marvels that this subtlety is part of the cathedral's design; but here Charpentier's knowledge is lacking. He fails to recognize that the ray descends from a window dedicated to Saint Apollinaris, a figure who at once belongs to the ranks of the Church, but whose name clearly indicates "Holy Apollo." Clearly what is on display here by combining sunlight and Apollo's name is not some formulation of heresy, but rather a belief that "Apollo is not the god of light but the Light of God."[139] Indeed, the dedication of this window strengthens Charpentier's interpretation of Chartres' geometry as Pythagorean, since Apollo is the ultimate source of the Pythagorean tradition, and the solstices are of particular importance in Pythagorean doctrine.[140]

In this context, then, we would do well to consider the Classical significance of the constellation that was chosen for the cathedrals' arrangement. Following Ovid, Latin poets relate that with the loss of the Golden Age of Saturn, the virgin Justice left the world to become the constellation Virgo; this maid is also called Astraea, a name emphasizing her stellar identity.[141] Her special relevance to the Christian world, however, derives from the Fourth Ecologue of Virgil:

> Now is come the last age of the Cumaean prophecy:

---

[139] Martin Lings, *The Sacred Art of Shakespeare*, Rochester: Inner Traditions, 1998, page 8.
[140] Pythagoras himself is depicted on an archivolt of the cathedral's western entrance.
[141] See Frances A. Yates, *Astraea: The Imperial Theme in the Sixteenth Century*, Middlesex: Peregrine Books, 1977, especially pages 30-5.

> The great cycle of periods is born anew.
> Now returns the Maid, returns the reign
>   of Saturn:
> Now from high heaven a new generation
>   comes down.
> Yet do thou at that boy's birth,
> In whom the iron race shall begin to
>   cease,
> And the golden to arise over all the
>   world,
> Holy Lucina, be gracious; now thine own
>   Apollo reigns.[142]

Beginning with the Emperor Constantine, the Maid comes to be identified with the Virgin Mary, just as the boy who signals the return of a Golden Age was understood to be Jesus. Even so, the prophecy of Virgil proceeds from the Cumaean Sybil, who serves Apollo, and Apollo himself is named by Virgil. The presence of Apollo in the design of Chartres may serve as a reminder, then, that the arrangement of cathedrals in the form of Astraea belongs to a harmonious plan aligned with the prophecy of Virgil.

∇

With this in mind, another element in the design of Chartres now appears to be a specific reference to Virgil, even if this significance has been overlooked. This element is the labyrinth, an ornate design laid out upon the floor of the cathedral at its western end. Charpentier barely mentions it, and so the causes for the modern worldwide distribution of the Chartres labyrinth design in particular is unlikely to derive from his book. As far as

---

[142] Ecologue 4, lines 4-11, translated by John William Mackail.

Virgil is concerned, a labyrinth figures in the sixth book or canto of the *Aeneid*, before the hero begins his journey to the Underworld. Aeneas undertakes this journey with the help of none other than the Cumaean Sybil, and he ponders the labyrinth as a design at the temple of Apollo. René Guénon explains: "Let us also recall that at Cumae the labyrinth was traced on the gates, as if this representation were in a certain way a substitute for the labyrinth itself; and it could be said that when Aeneas paused at the entrance to consider it, he in fact passed through the labyrinth mentally, if not bodily."[143] If such may be said of Aeneas, then no doubt this is applicable to the worshippers at Chartres, and so the interpretation of its labyrinth's purpose should not be restricted to the physical act of walking. For the worshippers at Chartres, however, the help of the Virgin Mary has replaced that of the Sybil.

While cathedral labyrinths are found outside the Gothic milieu, for example in Italy, it should nevertheless be observed that each of the principal cathedrals comprising the Virgo arrangement includes a labyrinth, with Reims, Bayeux, and Amiens following in the example of Chartres. Consequently, it may be offered that the writings of Virgil offer a source for both the symbolism of Astraea as well as the insistence on a labyrinth design. The relevance of these writings is clear enough through the existence of Medieval commentaries, such as a commentary on the *Aeneid* by a certain Bernardus. While debate surrounds whether Bernardus Silvestris or Bernard of Chartres is the author, it is nevertheless remarkable in the present context that there are ties to Chartres in either case. Moreover, the relevance of Cumae may even be detected in the fact that Bernardus' commentary ends midway through the sixth book, the very book that includes the labyrinth and Aeneas' journey to the Underworld.

---

[143] "The Cave and the Labyrinth," op. cit.

Concerning the designation "Underworld," it is important to avoid modern conceptions. In the Classical tradition, the Underworld is the Land of the Dead, and while it was localized under the earth, by no means should it be understood as comprising only inferior psychic states. According to Hesiod, at the close of the Golden Age, the Hyperboreans entered into the earth, and so their help was sought after through openings in the earth.[144] In "The Cave and the Labyrinth," René Guénon makes a distinction between the initiatic cave that corresponds to the heart, the center of the microcosm where both superior and inferior domains are accessed, and the labyrinth that properly surrounds it and guards the center. The passage of the labyrinth has in fact been rightly understood to represent a journey to the Holy Land, the "Heart of the World." What is not well understood is why both Theseus and the Minotaur have been depicted at the center of cathedral labyrinths, including, supposedly, the labyrinth at Chartres;[145] but this indicates well enough the position of the heart between possibilities both higher and lower, and serves as a reminder that only the qualified should be allowed to enter it. The purpose of a cathedral labyrinth thus follows that of the baptistry, the position of which

---

[144] The sanctity of the caverns associated with the Hyperborean Apollo in the environs of Mount Parnassus may very well relate to this notion, which should in turn be compared with the Celtic memory of the Tuatha Dé Danann and that of the "Ancient White People" among Native Americans. Cf. *The Red and the White*, op. cit.

[145] This depiction of Theseus and the Minotaur likely derived from Italian examples, and appeared upon a copper plate at the center of the design; this plate is said to have been preserved until 1792, its pagan iconography safeguarded within Christendom until the antitraditional upheavals of the French Revolution.

"precedes" the labyrinth at Chartres and that effects a kind of psychic preparation for the initiatic journey.[146]

These considerations become essential in evaluating the very special form and encoded numerology of the labyrinth at Chartres. The circle encompassing its design is framed by what have been termed "lunations," small crescent shapes that are unique to the design at Chartres. There are in fact no less than 113 "lunations," but one of them opens into two, in a sense, in order to accomodate the path. Now, the Holy Qur'an is comprised of 114 chapters, or *surahs*, of which the first is named "The Opening" (113+1). There are in this comparison a number of precise details to be observed. To begin with, while the term "lunation" is a modern one, it does describe the crescent shape of the divisions, and as I have explained elsewhere, the crescent is a far from arbitrary symbol of Islam.[147] More remarkably, the very term *"surah"* includes the meanings of "wall" or "rampart," that is, precisely what is being represented on the outside of the labyrinth. In Islamic esoterism in particular, the sequence of surahs is considered an "initiatory pathway" that mirrors in reverse the sequence in which they appear in the Qur'an. Of course, the labyrinth itself is nothing if not a pathway, and the way in is but the reverse of the way out. Knowledges pertaining to this pathway of the surahs constitute a whole section of the great work *Futūhāt al-Makkiyah* of the Greatest Master Muhyiddin Ibn ʿArabi, and the technical name for the stages along this path is *manāzil*.[148] *Manāzil*

---

[146] Guénon, "The Octagon," *Symbols of Sacred Science*, op. cit. For this reason, it is not without significance that many cathedral labyrinths, such as the one at Reims, are octagonal, like medieval baptistries.
[147] See *The Red and the White*, page 55.
[148] See the seminal work on this subject by Charles-André Gilis, *La clés des Demeures spirituelles dans les Futūhāt d'Ibn Arabî*, Paris: Éditions Traditionnelles, 1991. On page 69, the author even

is more commonly used to refer to the Lunar Mansions of astrology, so the use of *crescents* is strangely exact in this context.

There is more. The central space of the labyrinth contains a pattern of 6 inward-facing crescents, with trefoils marking their meeting points, and the number 6 indicates here the spiritual realization attainable through the center that, as mentioned above, corresponds to the heart.[149] Among the numbers present, it cannot be ignored that 6 is a factor of 114. The number revealed through dividing 114 by 6 is 19, and this number is of key importance in Islamic esoterism.[150] Correspondences between the structure of the world and of the microcosm as well as of the Holy Qur'an are based upon this number.[151] Specifically, 19 is the number of letters comprising the *basmala*, the sacred formula opening every surah of the Qur'an save one.[152] The numerical significance of this formula is moreover the subject of a Tradition of the Holy Prophet: "The one who desires immunity from the 19 Wardens of Hell needs to recite the *basmala*." In other words, 19 is fundamental to the soul's defense in a "land of the dead," even if Hell is not located under this world in Islamic cosmology. It is also true that

---

explains a context in which "The Opening" surah is considered apart from the 113 others.

[149] On the 6 powers of the heart in Islamic esoterism, see Shaykh Muhammad Hisham Kabbani, *The Sufi Science of Self-Realization*, Louisville: Fons Vitae, 2006.

[150] The number 19 is in fact explicitly indicated, albeit subtly, by the splitting of one of the trefoils due to the position of the path; the result is a total of 19 trefoil points (see diagram on page 78).

[151] Cf. "The Science of the Balance" in Henry Corbin, *Temple and Contemplation*, London: KPI Limited, 1986. 19 also relates to Apollonian tradition: according to Diodorus of Sicily, 19 years was the duration of Apollo's visit to the Hyperboreans.

[152] Even though only 113 surahs begin with the *basmala*, there is a 114th inclusion of the formula within surah XXVII where it is associated with Solomon.

if the Qur'an is to be opened and the *basmala* recited, this act must be preceded by the ritual of ablution (*wudu'*). The analogy with the baptistry preceding the passage of the labyrinth should be clear.[153]

As profound as these connections are, the presence of hidden Islamic elements at the heart of Chartres cathedral may seem unlikely; yet this scenario has a well-known literary equivalent. It has been over a century since the appearance of Miguel Asín Palacios *La Escatologia Musulmana en la Divina Comedia*, in which the author presented clear evidence that Christendom's greatest poem was modeled upon the Night Journey and Ascension (*isra' wal-mi`raj*) of the Prophet of Islam. In a similar way, even if the importance of Virgil at Chartres has been downplayed, this may never be so for Virgil in Dante's poem. René Guénon writes: "If Dante takes Virgil for his guide in the first two parts of his journey, the principal reason, as everyone recognizes, is doubtless his recollection of the sixth canto of the *Aeneid*, but we must add that this is because Virgil's work is no poetic fiction, but, on the contrary, gives incontestable proof of initiatic knowledge."[154]

In *The Esoterism of Dante*, Guénon explores the initiatory meanings expressed in *The Divine Comedy*, These meanings are expressed through the Pythagorean language of number, as is shown by the importance of the number 11[155] and its multiples in the poem's structure. We have had reason enough to consider the labyrinth at

---

[153] Another Tradition of the Prophet Muhammad teaches, "Ablution is the armament of the believer." Clearly this armament does not manifest in the physical domain.

[154] *The Esoterism of Dante*, Hillsdale: Sophia Perennis, 2001, page 26. Guénon observes that all three parts of Dante's poem end with the same word, *stelle*, that accords with the astrological context of Astraea's return (pages 33-4).

[155] The number 11 is of principal importance according to the Science of Letters (*`ilm al-hurūf*) in Islam, since it is the value of the name of the Divine Essence, *Hū*.

Chartres to be a memory of the Aeneid's sixth book, like the choice of Dante's guide, and it should also be observed that its structure is formed by precisely 11 circuits. If this number is multiplied by 6, the number geometrically expressed by the center of the labyrinth, the result is 66, a number likewise present in *The Divine Comedy*.[156] More curiously, just as the *Inferno* is composed of 34 cantos, so does the course of the labyrinth require 34 turns to reach the center. This last coincidence must be treated with caution, however, since Guénon warns against equating the passage of the labyrinth with the descent into Hell.[157] Recall that Aeneas passes the labyrinth *prior* to his descent, and we insisted above that accessing other domains requires that the center first be reached, just as Jerusalem is reached before Paradise and Hell during the miraculous Night Journey and Ascension. Dante was inspired by reports of this miracle, but his initial journey is instead dominated by the awareness of Hell. By reaching its center, however, he becomes aware of the axis aligned with Jerusalem that provides access to Hell, Purgatory, and Paradise. In any case, it should be admitted that the miraculous Night Journey to Jerusalem is even more directly related to the symbolism of the Chartres labyrinth, since, as Guénon reminds us, the passage of a cathedral labyrinth was traditionally considered to be a "substitute" for the pilgrimage to Jerusalem, the "Heart of the World."

Another number that shares its value with 11 and is of the greatest significance to Dante is the "palindrome-number" 515 (5+1+5=11). In *The Divine Comedy*, the person indicated by this number

> is accepted by most scholars, and generally taken as the image of "some

---

[156] The number 66 signifies nothing less than the "Supreme Identity" of Islamic esotericism. Cf. *The Symbolism of the Cross*, op. cit., page 18.
[157] "The Cave and the Labyrinth," op. cit.

hoped-for political saviour who would establish the just World-Empire"...This "God-sent" person seems to announce the prophetic advent of Jesus Christ at the end of the cycle and embodies...a divine figure made in the shape of a man, very close to the embodiment of Shaddai, the God of the Armies [as in Exodus (VI:1-3)], traditionally inscribed in the "shield of David" (*Maghen David*) or "seal of Solomon," and also related to the mysterious Angel of the Covenant, Metatron.[158]

We have already encountered this expectation expressed in Virgil's Fourth Ecologue as the reign of Apollo in a Golden Age necessarily attached to Jesus Christ. If the 11-circuit structure of the Chartres labyrinth relates to the number 515, so does its 6-fold central design relate to the Seal of Solomon.[159] Most significant of all, however, is the observation made by Charles-André Gilis, Guénon's continuator, that 515 is the numerical value in Arabic of the name "Idris,"[160] for Idris is Enoch, the antediluvian prophet of Abrahamic tradition explicitly associated with Metatron. Islamic esoterism regards Idris as the ever-living chief (*qutb*) of the spiritual hierarchy with a position corresponding to that of the Sun among the planets. While Idris may be said to embody the

---

[158] L. De Freitas, "515 – A Symmetric Number in Dante," *Computers & Mathematics with Applications*, volume 17 numbers 4-6, 1989, page 890.

[159] On the significance of 6 and its formulation as the Seal of Solomon, cf. René Guénon, *The Symbolism of the Cross*, Hillsdale: Sophia Perennis, 2001, chapter XXVIII.

[160] Cf. Charles-André Gilis, *Les Sept Étendards du Califat*, Paris: Éditions Traditionnelles, 1993, page 290. This calculation is based upon the value of letters according to the Western Abjad: 1+4+200+10+300=515.

Hyperborean tradition in a solar form, this description applies just as well to Apollo.[161]

In all this, then, there is evidence of an intellectual current to which the builders of Chartres and the author of *The Divine Comedy* both belonged, and that should properly be identified as Pythagorean.[162] Moreover, this current apparently depended upon the attachment of Christian esoterism to that of Islam. According to René Guénon, this was made possible through Dante's affiliation to a tertiary order of the Templars, which in turn accords with Charpentier's insistence upon the role of the Knights Templar at Chartres. In a real sense, the avowed role of the Order to guard pilgrims seeking the Holy Land corresponds exactly with the function of the labyrinth itself.[163] Just as the labyrinth safeguards the heart, those responsible for the design of Chartres guarded the source of their initiatory knowledge. Nevertheless, the Chartres labyrinth is in plain view, and part of a intelligible plan, since it is placed within a cathedral that itself belonged to a larger arrangement apparently representing the Virgo constellation; and while the guardians at Chartres were inviting Astraea to return to earth in accordance with the prophecy of Virgil, they no doubt anticipated the restoration of the Golden Age in the Christian and Islamic context of Jesus' return.

---

[161] On the Hyperborean Idris and Metatron, see *Sacred Geography and the Paths of the Sun*, page 39; on Apollo and Metatron, ibid., page 111; on Solomon and Metatron, ibid., page 79.

[162] "La filiation pythagoricienne de Virgile et de Dante est soulignée, dans l'œuvre de ces deux poètes, par la place toute spéciale qu'y occupe le dieu Apollon" (André Raeymaeker, "Les Fondements Pythagoriciens de l'Empire," *Études Traditionnelles*, number 440, Paris, 1973).

[163] From this perspective, the cruciform aspect of the Chartres labyrinth suggests the stamp of the Templars, whose emblem was a "footed" cross pattée. Cf. *The Red and the White*, page 81.

The Labyrinth of the Age of Gold

∇

The Grail legends first appear in Europe during the same period as Chartres' construction. This historical formulation of the Grail presents a convergence of three elements: a pre-Christian Celtic foundation, a Christian setting, and an inspiration proceeding from Islamic esoterism.[164] In a comparable threefold manner, as we have seen, the pre-Christian Classical motif of the labyrinth appears in a Christian setting at Chartres and displays indications likewise proceeding from Islam. Of course, in the case of the Grail and the Chartres labyrinth alike, the role of Islam has been routinely overlooked, yet this is perhaps to be expected, given esoterism's hidden character. However, regarding the Grail, rather sinister influences have usurped the role of Islamic esoterism in more recent formulations.

As for the Chartres labyrinth, it is worth considering in more detail its recent and wide distribution that was alluded to above. The practice of walking a labyrinth would seem to belong to the counter-traditional developments of the "New Age." Regarding the design of the Chartres labyrinth in particular, however, a transfer of sorts was accomplished within the context of established Christianity. In 1991, a group led by Dr. Lauren Artress from America purposely walked the labyrinth in Chartres cathedral, in order to then establish an exact copy within the Episcopal cathedral in San Francisco, California.[165] This copy, at first temporary

---

[164] Cf. *Sacred Geography and the Paths of the Sun*, page 89.

[165] Lauren Artress is a minister as well as a psychotherapist, and the demands of the latter may have attracted her to the labyrinth's utility in psychic defense. She reports of her initial experience at Chartres: "I received the embrace of Mary." (*Walking a Sacred Path: Rediscovering the Labyrinth as a Spiritual Tool*, New York: Riverhead Books, 1995, page 6). Her name, it should be noted, refers to laurel, the sacred plant of Apollo.

and then permanent, is the source of a phenomenon: two-dimensional labyrinth designs large enough to walk have now been placed throughout the world, in secular as well as Christian settings. An internet site calculates their number at some 6000. Of course, it is unknown what percentage of these have been modelled upon the labyrinth at Chartres, though it surely represents a majority; and even those modelled after Chartres are not necessarily exact copies, since they may vary in the number of circuits, or by the absence of lunations, etc.

I have had occasion in *Mysteries of Dune* to compare San Francisco and its Golden Gate with Constantinople and its Golden Horn, observing that the former deliberately copied the name from the latter. I also noted that "both Constantinople and San Francisco are recognized as occupying sites having seven hills, and both are identified by locals simply as 'the City,' as the modern name of Istanbul (literally, 'to the city') made official."[166] Of course, the model of the city upon seven hills is Rome, and it also pertains to our subject, with Virgil's *Aeneid* ultimately providing an account of Rome's founding. It may also be recalled that Constantine, the eponymous founder of East Rome, was the first to offer a Christian interpretation for Virgil's Fourth Ecologue.[167] When the Ottomans conquered Constantinople, they inherited the title of Caesar, yet still looked forward to the eschatological conquest of Rome proper. This eschatological Rome was known as the "Red Apple (*kizil elma*)," although the designation was applied to other cities, such as Constantinople before its conquest, as well as Vienna that the Ottomans failed to conquer, or even Cologne in Germany, for reasons that needn't detain us here.

---

[166] *Mysteries of Dune: Sufism, Psychedelics, and the Prediction of Frank Herbert*, Temple of Justice Books, 2020, page 67.

[167] Recall that the Emperor Constantine relocated the so-called Serpent Column from the Temple of Apollo in Delphi to his capital, where it remained through the Ottoman period.

The Labyrinth of the Age of Gold

What is certainly worth considering, however, is that Islamic esoterism depicts this eschatological Rome as a labyrinth. The labyrinthine "City Talisman" in various forms appears in the writings of the Shaykh al-Akbar Muhyiddin Ibn `Arabi,[168] the very master whose teachings on the sequence of surahs was referenced earlier. The discovery of another reason to acknowledge this source should not be too surprising. After all, the *Futuhat al-Makkiyah* of Shaykh Muhyiddin has long been singled out as being among the likeliest of Dante's sources, whether direct or not; and René Guénon admits that "we have many reasons to think that to a considerable extent Dante indeed was inspired by the writings of Muhyi 'd-Dīn."[169] Guénon observes that these writings precede Dante's by some 80 years, and this estimate coincides more or less exactly with the construction of the cathedral labyrinth at Chartres. Given its features that bear the imprint of Islamic esoterism and the Shaykh al-Akbar in particular, this labyrinth appears more than superficially related to the City Talisman of the Akbarian tradition. Remarkably, the City Talisman labels the center of the labyrinth as *qalb*, the heart, thus insisting upon the correspondence between the microcosm and the sacred city of the macrocosm;[170] and even though the talisman indicates a progression into the more subtle

---

[168] See Gerald T. Elmore, *Islamic Sainthood in the Fullness of Time: Ibn al-`Arabī's Book of the Fabulous Gryphon*, Leiden: Brill, 1999, pages 587-8; the English term "City Talisman" is from Elmore.

[169] *The Esoterism of Dante*, op. cit., page 29. Although his spiritual function was absolutely unique, his teachings could be considered Neopythagorean; he was in fact recognized as Ibn Iflatun, the "Son of Plato." On Pythagoras and Plato as followers of the Apollonian tradition, see *Sacred Geography and the Paths of the Sun*, page 27.

[170] Cf. Guénon on the "Divine City:" "We know that what is properly designated by this is the center of the being, represented by the heart, which moreover effectively corresponds to it in the corporeal organism" ("The Divine City," *Symbols of Sacred Science*, op. cit., page 443).

degrees of the being (*lata'if*) in an outward direction, this is easily accounted for in terms of the reversal described earlier with regards to the "initiatory pathway" and the order of surahs.[171]

The writings of Virgil concern the beginning of Rome; the Shaykh al-Akbar illuminates its end. Shaykh Muhyiddin associates the conquest of the eschatological Rome with the rightly-guided leader whose appearance belongs in Islam to the "major signs" of the Apocalypse.[172] This leader is named al-Mahdi in the Traditions, according to which his function is inseparable from and preparatory to the return of Jesus. In terms of the foregoing, the description of the one to "announce the prophetic advent of Jesus Christ at the end of the cycle" applies perfectly to him. The Shaykh al-Akbar also calls him the "Sun of the West," and since his role is linked to Jesus, this immediately recalls the Christian liturgical focus upon the Sun toward the east, as evidenced by the literal "orientation" of Medieval churches.[173] Now, in East and West the symbol of the Sun is a circle with its center marked. In the most fundamental terms, the Chartres Labyrinth may be so described. Charles-André Gilis makes reference to this symbol in describing the roles of al-Mahdi and Jesus,[174] associating each with a half-circumference of the circle, even while insisting that the complete symbol clearly indicates the solar domain of Idris. It may also be observed that it is the polar axis that defines the complementary terms of east and west, and that this polar axis is what is being indicated by the term "Hyperborean," as well, of course, by the Arabic title *qutb*

---

[171] It is also worth noting that the word *qalb* literally means "reversal," and that its numerical value is 132, that is, twice the number 66.

[172] In Arabic, to "conquer" is literally to "open," and this accords with the etymology of the word "apocalypse."

[173] This orientation is given a scriptural basis in Matthew 24: 27 that is understood to refer to the Second Coming.

[174] Op. cit. 1993, pages 289-90.

The Labyrinth of the Age of Gold

or "Pole" for the chief of the spiritual hierarchy. Be that as it may, the symbol for the Sun is likewise the symbol for gold, and Christianity and Islam must be seen as united in belief in a coming Age of Gold under Jesus.

If the labyrinth of Chartres may function as a City Talisman of the Apocalypse,[175] then its duplication – or rather projection - in cities around the world is a development of great interest, especially since this projection began in San Francisco, a city between East and West[176] patterned in some measure after Rome. If it serves a talismanic purpose, its precise duplication must be a matter of essential importance. With its focus upon the heart, the design is complete in itself, and does not require placement in a church, even if it was safeguarded for centuries within Chartres cathedral. Again, the walking of the labyrinth is not essential to its purpose, and if modern examples depart from the proper form, then the more meaningless must be such activity. Even so, the one and only course to the center offers reassurance to anyone who watches their feet upon the path. The Cumaean prophecy foretells "the golden to arise over all the world," and perhaps the worldwide distribution of the Chartres labyrinth is a sign of this spiritualization of the macrocosm; and if so, the mystery of 19 letters is essential to the return of Apollo's reign and the Second Coming of Jesus.

---

[175] If the single entrance into the center of the labyrinth is added to the number 6 that is depicted there, the sum is 7, and it is possible to see in this a reference to the seven hills of Rome. For his part, the Catholic author J.R.R. Tolkien would depict his Rome at the end of an age as a seven-walled labyrinthine city (see *Alchemy in Middle-earth: The Significance of J.R.R. Tolkien's The Lord of the Rings*, Temple of Justice Books, 2003, page 40).

[176] Cf. *The Red and the White*, page 76. Saint Francis, after whom the city was named, is widely recognized as having participated in a reconciliation of Christianity and Islam.

***Portrait of the Emperor Solymannus (Sulaiman)
of the Ottomans***
from the *Armamentarium Heroicum* of Austrian Archduke
Frederick II

∇

The Lost Ottoman Heart
of Europe

Beginning in 2013 and continuing occasionally for some years, a series of news articles circulated widely concerning a macabre historical mystery. On the BBC for example, the title, "The Search for Suleiman the Magnificent's Heart" summarized what was unfolding in an obscure town in southern Hungary. Archaeologists were claiming to have located a site associated with the passing of the Ottoman Sultan who was known as the Lawgiver, but who was better known in Christian Europe as "the Magnificent." Sultan Sulaiman had died from natural causes while on military campaign in 1566. The location where he had died has been forgotten, but an Ottoman shrine complex marking the site had once crowned a hill above the swamplands near Szigetvár. The complex had been known simply as Turbék, after the Ottoman word for "tomb," even though a tomb belonging to the sultan was established also in his capital of Constantinople. The latter housed his body, whereas it was believed that the internal organs, and particularly the heart, of the celebrated sultan had been interred within the shrine in Hungary. Although once a purported pilgrimage site, it had been razed a little more than a century after its establishment, and so its precise location had been obscured. However, pilgrimage continued to the area in later years following an apparition of the Virgin Mary in 1705; in fact, it was assumed that the Turbéki Catholic church was the former location of the Ottoman shrine, although archaeologists have now determined that this assumption was incorrect.

By virtue of the conquest of Constantinople in 1453, the Ottomans had become the renewers of the Holy Roman Empire. For them, to the west was Rumelia, land of the Romans, and they hoped to complete their conquest in the west. They were opposed in their efforts, of course, by another claimant to the rule of the Holy Roman Empire, the Catholic House of Hapsburg, who was responsible for the razing of Turbék. Now, these competing claims were based in the Medieval division of the empire into eastern and western domains, but the 16th century brought further division to the western empire in the form of the Protestant Revolution. Of course, authority over the western empire had been long contested between emperors and the Papacy. In his work on the principles of sacred geography and the proper authority presiding over it, *The King of the World*, René Guénon observes: "Such a separation can be considered the mark of an organization that is incomplete at its summit, so to speak, since there we do not find the common principle from which the two powers regularly proceed and on which they depend, the true supreme power having therefore to be sought elsewhere;" and in a footnote, he explains: "The Islamic theory of the Caliphate also unites the two powers." [177] The Mamluks of Egypt had safeguarded the caliphal legacy following the Mongol destruction of the caliph's former seat of Baghdad; but Sulaiman's predecessor Salim had in fact inherited the title of Caliph by virtue of his victory over the Mamluks in 1519. Of course, in the case of Sulaiman, the Ottoman emperor also happened to be the namesake of the "common principle" of authority for Jews,

---

[177] Op. cit., page 9.

Christians, and Muslims alike, the priest-king Solomon, and so he was hailed as a Second Solomon. No doubt his empire embraced Jews, Christians, and Muslims.

By the 16th century, Ottoman sources refer to the goal of military conquest as the "Red Apple (*kizil elma*)." It became the custom for the Ottoman ruler at his investiture to greet the head of his Janissary bodyguard with the formulaic expression, "We shall meet at the Red Apple." Very likely, the imagery derived from the ultimate goal of the "greater" Rome (*rūm al-kubra*), the conquest of which was expected to follow the apocalyptic appearance of the leader called al-Mahdi.[178] More immediately, the name "Red Apple" was understood to apply to other cities upon which the Ottomans set their sights, such as Budapest and Vienna; yet even the distant Cologne in Germany was among the cities so named. Sultan Sulaiman personally commanded his armies on campaign, and laid siege to Vienna for the first time in 1529; Budapest was conquered in 1541. He was praised as the "Owner of the Fortunate Conjunction" (*sāhib al-qirān*), a title principally attached to the memory of the greatest of conquerors, Alexander the Great. Not without good reason, Sulaiman's conquests suggested a messianic fulfillment. At the dawning of the tenth century of the Islamic calendar, Sulaiman was in fact the tenth ruler of the Ottoman house, and so the "Perfector of the Perfect Number."[179] For the Ottomans, he was nothing less than "the ruler of the Last Age, whose universal dominion and enforcement of the universal victory of Islam is to precede

---

[178] Cf. F.W. Hasluck, "The Prophecy of the Red Apple," in *Christianity and Islam Under the Sultans*, volume II, Oxford: Oxford University Press, 1929. On al-Mahdi and Rome, cf. "The Labyrinth of the Age of Gold."
[179] Cf. my *Sacred Geography and the Paths of the Sun*, page 122.

directly the advent of the Mahdi and the descent of Jesus."[180]

Alexander the Great is named in the Holy Qur'an as Dhul-Qarnayn, "that is, 'of the two horns,' which is most frequently interpreted in the sense of a double power extending over both the East and the West."[181] As a Second Alexander, Sultan Sulaiman indeed exercised an authority over the East and the West. The principal emblem of his Eastern conquests was the so-called "Cup of Jamshid," that in fact had belonged to Alexander, and that was regarded as the embodiment of Persian sovereignty.[182] In the European West, there should be little doubt that the shrine for the heart of Sultan Sulaiman is the emblem of his Western authority. It is perhaps worth pointing out that René Guénon repeatedly insists on the equivalence between the symbolism of the cup and that of the heart.[183]

There is, however, another tomb for a sultan's heart in Europe, and it belongs to the only other Ottoman ruler to have died while on campaign. The tomb of Sultan Murad in the fields of Kosova provides a fortunate precedent for the policy undertaken in Hungary, even if the sultan was not also caliph. Upon the sultan's martyrdom in 1389, the heart and other vital organs were likewise removed before his body was returned to the earlier Ottoman capital of Bursa, and so two tombs also exist for Sultan Murad. The tomb of this martyr in Kosova might be compared with other Ottoman tombs that exist in relative isolation in the Balkans and that belong to the Sufi saints, such as the heptagonal tombs of the Abdal

---

[180] Cornell H. Fleischer, "Seer to the Sultan: Haydar-i Remmal and Sultan Süleyman," *Cultural Horizons*, New York: Syracuse University Press, 2001, page 296.

[181] René Guénon, "The Symbolism of Horns," *Symbols of Sacred Science*, op. cit.

[182] Cf. *Sacred Geography and the Paths of the Sun*, page 122.

[183] See for example "The Sacred Heart and the Legend of the Holy Grail" in *Symbols of Sacred Science*.

that were among the subjects of *Sacred Geography and the Paths of the Sun*. In Turbék, however, the tomb structure was square, apparently, and so not like the octagonal tomb for the sultan's body in Constantinople, nor even like the tomb for Sultan Murad's heart in Kosova. What is more, the shrine in Hungary was not only a tomb structure or even complex, but a whole settlement, and it is this characteristic that is unique in the Balkans. What the Ottomans undertook upon the hill near Szigetvár was the construction of a town from nothing, unlike their practice of improving already existing settlements; and this town was moreover uniquely dedicated to the sanctity of the sultan. More precisely, the town existed as a container for the heart or *coeur* – and therefore the essential core – of the authority he embodied.

Recent news reports describe the settlement: "...between 1573 and 1577 a fortified 'holy town' was built around the tomb, comprising two mahalla or districts, home initially to around 50 households – probably the families of the soldiers guarding it. Over the following decades, the town grew in importance, and an inn, two mosques, a Dervish lodge and baths were built for the many pilgrims and visitors."[184] It is worth insisting how these establishments comprised

---

[184] Nick Thorpe, "Search for Suleiman's Heart Reveals a Whole Town," BBC News, 23 September 2013.

an integrated whole. For example, the spiritual authority at Turbék was known as the "Shaykh of the Tomb" (*seyhü't-türbe*), a title affirming his role as a Sufi master, and even if a dervish lodge is the base for a master's training of souls, the shaykh and his dervishes would still be required to pray in the mosques. One of the most illustrious Bosnian Sufis of the 16th century is known to have served in this capacity, Shaykh `Ali Dede from Mostar. His master in turn was the Shaykh Nureddin-zade Musliheddin Mustafa, the master of the Halveti Order who had accompanied Sultan Sulaiman on his last campaign;[185] in other words, this shaykh at least was also a soldier. Of course, the attachment of the Ottoman Janissaries to the Bektashi Order is well known.[186] Concerning the Halveti Order specifically, it is worth observing that the Ottoman military of this period was attached especially to a Halveti master from Egypt, Ibrahim Gülsheni.[187] It may be presumed, then, that the guardians of the tomb were attached to the same order and so belonged to the same lodge as the Shaykh of the Tomb. At the very least, it should be recognized that military or temporal power and dervish training were united under the caliphal authority of the heart of Turbék, the embodiment of "the common principle from which the two powers regularly proceed."

As Turbék "grew in importance," it is worth observing that the number of guardians assigned to the

---

[185] Gabor Ágoston, "Muslim Cultural Enclaves in Hungary under Ottoman Rule," *Acta Orientalia Academiae Scienciarum Hungaricae*, volume 45, 1991, pages 198-9.

[186] It is worth noting that the spiritual affiliation of the Janissaries, the "Sons of Hajji Bektash," is sometimes traced to Sultan Murad's martyrdom in Kosova. See Cf. F.W. Hasluck, "Hajji Bektash and the Janissaries," op. cit.

[187] Cf. B.G. Martin, "A Short History of the Khalwati Order of Dervishes," *Scholars, Saints, and Sufis: Muslim Religious Institutions in the Middle East since 1500*, edited by Keddie, Berkeley: University of California Press, 1972, page 296.

tomb did not grow accordingly,[188] and so there must have been a significance to their number. René Guénon briefly considers the significance of the number 50 in relation to another knightly company, that of King Arthur: "The 'Knights of the Round Table' sometimes number 50 (which for the Hebrews was the number of the Jubilee, and which was also related to the 'reign of the Holy Spirit')."[189] Elsewhere he mentions the number as being the value of the Arabic letter Nūn, that is, the letter at the end of the name "Sulaiman." Guénon explains that the shape of this letter "is a schematic equivalent of the cup," and he continues by relating this to the symbolism of the heart.[190] It is at least curious, then, that the role of these "guardians of the heart" at Turbék should be so comparable to that of the knights who guard the sacred cup of Arthurian lore.[191] It is also significant in this context that Islamic esoterism regards the number 50 to be essentially equivalent to 5,[192] and the apotropaic value of 5, as well as its Pythagorean formulation as the pentagram, is too well established to review here.

When the Ottomans inherited the caliphate, they inherited also the caliphal relics that were transferred to Constantinople. As an expression of vigilance, continuous sacred invocation would be observed in the

---

[188] Ágoston, page 198.
[189] *The King of the World*, op. cit., page 31.
[190] "The Mysteries of the Letter Nūn," *Symbols of Sacred Science*, op. cit.
[191] The comparison is especially apt in the case of the templars of the "sacred isle" of Montsalvasche in the *Parzival* of Wolfram von Eschenbach. If it is countered that the Grail is not a cup but a stone in that work, it should be observed that the letter Nūn is formed by both a cup and a dot, and that this dot holds a very comparable significance to the sacred stone in Islamic esoterism. It is also worth noting that these templars were named for the historical Order of the Temple of Solomon, who, like the dervish guardians of Turbék, defended a "Solomonic" inheritance.
[192] Cf. Ibn Arabî, *Le Livre du Mîm, du Wâw et du Nûn*, presented by Charles-André Gilis, Beirut: Albouraq, 2002, page 65.

presence of these relics. There is every reason to presume that such an expression of vigilance would have been accomplished in turns by the dervish guardians of the heart. This practice may be compared with that "most powerful ally of priestcraft," the "perpetual sacred chant" that John Michell compares with the "weaving of a spell."[193] The contemporary Ottoman savant Evliya Çelebi was instructed in the art of the "mystical chant" by a Halveti master, and the practice of sacred music and dance was indeed a particularity of that order.[194] Despite this, the holy town of Turbék was razed to the ground by Habsburg forces when they captured nearby Szigetvár in 1692. There is no historical account of the fate of the dervish guardians of Turbék, nor indeed of the sacrosanct treasure they served to protect.

▽

In *Sacred Geography and the Paths of the Sun*, I considered ancient doctrines relating to the fate of the soul and addressed how these doctrines are still given expression upon the landscapes of Europe. In particular, the location of Constantinople in relation to Mount Parnassus figured in this discussion, since the former lies upon a solar azimuth from the sacred mountain. This azimuth is fact corresponds to the sunrise upon the summer solstice; for the Pythagoreans, who specialized in these matters, the solstices were gateways for souls entering and exiting this world. Now, what is truly remarkable in this context is that the hill of Turbék lies precisely upon the azimuth of the summer solstice sunset

---

[193] John Michell and Christine Rhone, *Twelve-Tribe Nations and the Science of Enchanting the Landscape*, London: Thames and Hudson, 1991, pages 68-70.
[194] Cf. Martin, op. cit.

from Constantinople. In other words, the mortal remains of Sultan Sulaiman were linked by a "path of the Sun" that belonged to the Pythagorean mysteries of death. If the likelihood of such mysteries surviving in an Islamic milieu seems remote, we must recall the comparable example of the Axis of Saint Michael and Apollo in Christian Europe, as well as the vitality of Pythagoreanism within both Christian and Islamic esoterisms. In fact, according to the latter, the wisdom of Pythagoras is attached to the authority of the prophet Sulaiman in particular, a not insignificant detail in the present context.

It is at least worth examining whether there are any other sites of interest bound together by this alignment, and indeed there are (pages 106-7). Proceeding towards the summer solstice sunset from Constantinople, one of the aforementioned tombs of the Abdal, that of Kidemli Baba, is found situated upon its own "Island Hill" (*Ada Tepe*) in Bulgaria. Only a very few of these heptagonal monuments were built, all before the time of Sultan Sulaiman, so to find this architectural testament to the saintly hierarchy here is surely not without significance.[195] Further to the northwest, the Serbian city of Belgrade lies exactly on the alignment; Sultan Sulaiman conquered this city on his push westward in 1521, and it mostly remained in Ottoman hands for centuries. Most significant of all, however, is that if the line is extended so that Turbék is at its center, the alignment reaches to the German city of Aachen. With its Palatine Chapel, Aachen was the ceremonial home of the Holy Roman Empire in the West, and so represents a

---

[195] On the heptagonal monuments of the Abdal, see *Sacred Geography and the Paths of the Sun*, chapter 5. It should not be overlooked that the title of the saint, "Kidemli," is from the Arabic root q-d-m that is of special relevance to the matter of ancient "pathways;" cf. *The Red and the White*, page 69.

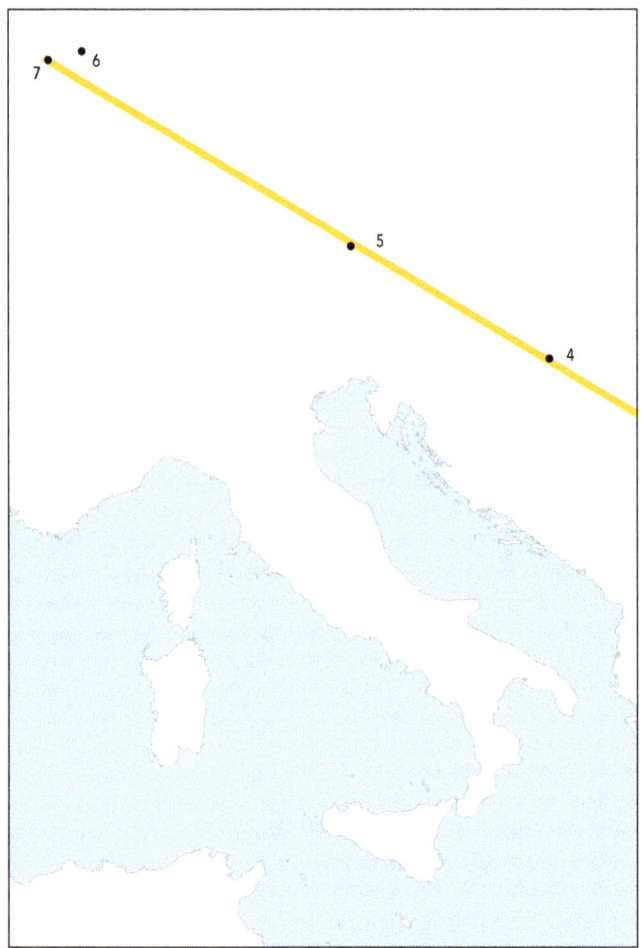

The Kizil Elma Alignment

    1   Constantinople
    2   Kidemli Baba
    3   Belgrade

The Lost Ottoman Heart of Europe

4   Turbék
5   Salzburg
6   Cologne
7   Aachen

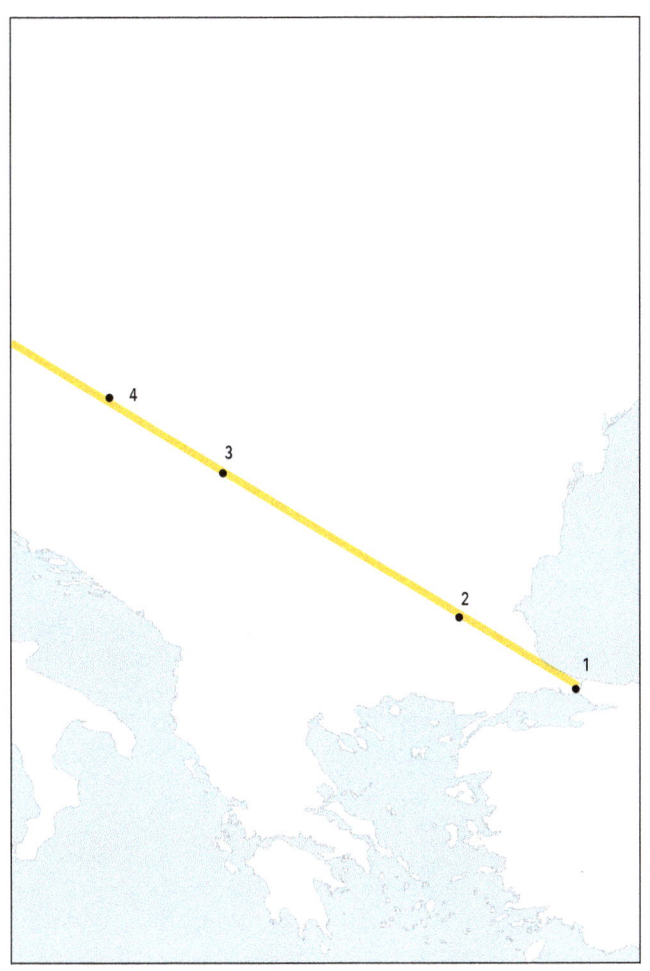

kind of western counterpart to the capital of the Holy Roman Empire in Constantinople. When Charlemagne was proclaimed emperor in 800 C.E., a Holy Roman Emperor was created in Rome despite the continued existence of the Holy Roman Emperor in Constantinople. The city of Aachen was built as a "Second Rome" far from the Pope, and to accommodate Charlemagne's tomb. The Palatine Chapel in Aachen Cathedral served as the coronation site for his successors throughout the Middle Ages. It is worth emphasizing that the location of Aachen was deliberately chosen. Ancient Rome had developed the site because of its thermal springs, and so the site would have been valued earlier still. The octagonal palace chapel was in fact positioned over the Roman baths, but its construction was also concerned with the celestial world: "At noon on June 21, the summer solstice, a ray of light fell directly upon the golden ball hanging from the chapel's domed ceiling, where the 'Barbarossa chandelier' depicts the heavenly Jerusalem." Moreover, on the same day, a ray of light would have illuminated the crown of the emperor as he sat on the throne.[196] In keeping with traditional symbolism, then, the throne of the emperor was placed between the lower world of the hot springs and the upper world of the Sun. Above all, however, we must recognize that by following the summer solstice sunset we have reached a complex deliberately illuminated by this same Sun.

It is strange, perhaps, that this "Second Rome" with its illumined golden orb was not identified as the most distant Kizil Elma; that distinction instead belongs to the neighboring city of Cologne. Prior to the rise of the Ottomans, the relics of the Three Magi were transferred

---

[196] Geoffrey Cornelius and Paul Devereux, *The Secret Language of the Stars and Planets*, San Francisco: Chronicle Books, 1996, pages 165. It is probably best not to attribute too much significance to the "Heavenly Jerusalem" reference; after all, the only doctrinal justification for a *Christian* emperor would derive from Jesus' apocalyptic return, when he displays royal power.

from Milan to Cologne in 1164, and its great cathedral was built specifically to house them. Thanks to René Guénon, we are able to identify the Three Magi as representatives of the three dimensions of sacred authority; we have already quoted him referring to these dimensions as the "two powers" and their "common principle." Of the three, the magus associated with the temporal domain must be considered here:

> According to John of Hildesheim, Melchior, the "smallest in stature," brought gold as his offering – including the treasure of Alexander the Great and "all the ornaments that the Queen of Saba (Sheba) offered in Solomon's temple." Among Alexander's treasures was a golden apple..."[197]

The relics in Cologne do not include these gifts, however, and what remains of the relics of the Magi were lessened further when some were reportedly returned to Milan in the first years of the 20th century. Still, the legacies of Solomon and Alexander the Great here are certainly relevant to the present context, and the mention of a golden apple in the context of Melchior's authority may very well be the source of the identification of Cologne with the Kizil Elma.

It is worth recalling that gold is the metal of the Sun, and that in the human microcosm, it is the heart that corresponds to the Sun.[198] In Hungary, stories had been told of the heart of Sultan Sulaiman being interred in a golden reliquary, but though the archaeologists reportedly found the foundations of the tomb in Turbék, they could find no trace of the heart. Still, the solar

---

[197] Caroline Stone, "We Three Kings of Orient Were," *Saudi Aramco World*, November/December 1980.
[198] Cf. for example Abu Bakr Sirāj ad-Dīn, *The Book of Certainty*, Cambridge: Islamic Texts Society, 1992.

alignment upon the landscape remains. An alignment would always have existed between Constantinople and Aachen, of course, even if it has never been recognized. The positioning of the tomb at Turbék, at the midpoint or heart of the whole alignment, is providential at least. In relation to this point of balance, however, the German and Ottoman claims to Empire do not seem equivalent; in fact, after some seven centuries, the imperial coronations at Aachen ceased in 1531, that is, during the reign of Sultan Sulaiman, and with the investiture of his last effective Habsburg rival, Charles V. It is perhaps more important to recall the "perpetual sacred chant" mentioned above, given the musical emphasis of Pythagoreanism that we have elsewhere seen expressed in the proportions of landscape alignments.[199] The benefit of ritual at the center of the alignment may easily be imagined to reverberate throughout its entire length. The importance of Turbék may also be compared with Mount Gargano at the midpoint of the Axis of Saint Michael and Apollo. Curiously, at both midpoints, there has been an "apparition," of the Virgin Mary at Turbék and of Saint Michael at Gargano; and since both holy figures belong to the traditions of Christianity and Islam alike, their appearance demonstrates a remarkable doctrinal balance, so to speak.

Having established the Pythagorean relevance of these solstitial alignments, it should be further observed that according to Herodotus, the teachings of Pythagoras concerning the fate of the soul derive from his time in Egypt. Of course, concerning the physical body, funerary practices involving the removal of the vital organs may be found in ancient Egypt as well, but the Ottoman burial should not be conflated with mummification. More relevant comparisons, perhaps, could be made with Medieval European examples of the separate burial of a ruler's heart and body, such as the mysterious example of

---

[199] See *Sacred Geography and the Paths of the Sun*, chapter 4.

Scotland's Robert the Bruce that I considered in *Alchemy in Middle-earth*.[200] Still, knowledge of ancient Egypt in Islamic esoterism is undeniable, as is clear in the life and teachings of the very great Sufi Dhun-Nūn of Egypt. A defense of this saint was written by the alchemist 'Uthman bin Suwayd, who was also the source for the Latin *Turba Philosophorum* in which Pythagoras appears.[201] In addition, the title of Ibn Suwayd's *Book of the Red Sulphur* exemplifies the adoption of alchemical terminology within Islamic esoterism, as does the use of the term *al-kimiya* itself. More than this, however, alchemical processes became practiced within Sufism, and within the Halveti Order in particular. Among its Egyptian masters, the shaykh Shahin al-Khalwati "was much concerned with 'alchemical manipulations,' which alienated him, according to al-Nabulusi."[202]

A strange story concerning alchemy during the reign of Sultan Sulaiman is told of the Christian alchemist Paracelsus: "In 1521 a Tatar prince took Paracelsus along with him on a diplomatic mission to Constantinople. There he allegedly met the magus who gave him the Philosopher's Stone." Paracelsus reportedly kept his "greatest treasure" in the hollow pommel of a sword "from which he never parted, not even in sleep."[203] In a

---

[200] Op. cit., pages 72-4. Curiously, shortly before the razing of Turbék, the interring of the heart apart from the body becomes a Habsburg tradition, with no less than 54 hearts being kept in the Herzgruft in Vienna.

[201] Cf. Peter Kingsley, "From Pythagoras to the Turba Philosophorum: Egypt and Pythagorean Tradition," *Journal of the Warburg and Courtauld Institute*, volume 57, 1994.

[202] Martin, op. cit., page 291.

[203] Quotations from Henry M. Pachter, *Paracelsus: Magic Into Science, being the True History of the Troubled Life, Adventures, Doctrines, Miraculous Cures, and Prophecies of the Most Renowned, Widely Traveled, Very Learned and Pious Gentleman, Scholar, and Most Highly Experienced and Illustrious Physicus, the Honorable Philippus Theophrastus Aureolus Bombastus Ab Hohenheim,*

portrait made of him less than a year before his passing, Paracelsus is indeed holding a sword, with its large spherical pommel held uppermost (at left). Now, the Philosopher's Stone is usually synonymous with the aforementioned "Red Sulphur;" around this time, when Dr. John Dee acquired the Philosopher's Stone from the ruins of England's Glastonbury Abbey, it is described as a red substance such as could likely be stored in a hollow pommel.[204] Paracelsus adopted alchemical teachings from the Islamic world, especially concerning the complementary forces of Sulphur and Mercury, but further insisted upon a third term, Salt. For Paracelsus, Sulphur, Mercury, and Salt were the Tria Prima, three principles not to be confused with the mundane substances by those names.[205] In any case, in the very year of his passing, Paracelsus moved to Salzburg in Austria, where his tomb may today be found; and in light of his teaching, according to which Salt corresponds to the physical body, it is worth acknowledging that "Salzburg" means "Fortress of Salt."

That is not all. The word "pommel" for the end of a sword hilt derives from the word for "apple" (*pomme* in French), due to its shape, and so a pommel containing the Philosopher's Stone suggests a rather extraordinary "red apple," or in the language of the city where the Stone was

---

Eremita, Called Paracelsus, New York: Schuman, 1951, pages 95-6.
[204] Cf. *Sacred Geography and the Paths of the Sun*, page 90.
[205] Cf. "Sulphur, Mercury, Salt" in René Guénon, *The Great Triad*, Hillsdale: Sophia Perennis, 2001.

obtained, *kizil elma*. What is more, though it should hardly by now be surprising, the city of Salzburg lies upon the solstitial alignment from Constantinople. Another striking coincidence presents itself: upon his tomb is a passage from the Book of Job, while the investiture of the Ottoman caliph was accomplished at the tomb of Job (*Ayyub Sultan*)[206], and this investiture was accomplished not with a crown, but with a sacred sword. However, like the heart of Sulaiman following the razing of Turbék, there is no further trace of the sword of Paracelsus.[207]

∇

For Paracelsus, the Tria Prima is at the foundation of all manifested forms. In the domain of sacred authority, there is a comparable three-fold expression, as we have seen in the archetypal example of the Three Magi. Again, the golden apple of Melchior is the emblem of temporal power, and the Kizil Elma was the goal of all temporal conquest for the Ottomans; among the Tria Prima, temporal power corresponds to Salt. Of the Three Magi, it is the one who offers myrrh who corresponds to the Red Sulphur, since myrrh is the "balm of incorruptibility, symbol of *Amrita*."[208] Still, all three powers must be present in the constitution of the traditional centers of sacred geography. In Turbék, it may be observed that spiritual authority and temporal power

---

[206] This Job (Ayyub) is the Companion of the Holy Prophet of Islam, properly Abu Ayyub al-Ansari, indirectly named for the Judaic prophet.

[207] In 1567, a portrait of Paracelsus comparable to that of 1540 includes the word "Azoth" written upon the pommel of his sword. This word is supposed to derive from the Arabic *az-zā'uq*, or Mercury, but its similarity to the word "azimuth" – from the Arabic word for "way" – is worth noting.

[208] *The King of the World*, op. cit., page 24.

were well represented by the knights and dervishes of the holy town; yet in the company of the heart, the dervish guardians also came to reflect "the common principle from which the two powers regularly proceed."[209]

The Shaykh al-Akbar of Islamic esoterism, Muhyiddin Ibn `Arabi, is known as the Red Sulphur, and he himself refers to this rank in an oft-quoted declaration in his *Kitab al-Isra* ("Book of the Night Journey"): "I desire to reach the City of the Messenger. I search for the Station of Radiancy and the Red Sulphur."[210] In his commentary on these words, Charles-André Gilis explains that the name "City of the Messenger" for Medina in Arabia includes the idea of Holy Empire. No doubt this accords with the symbolism of the heart of the Ottoman caliph who represents the Messenger. What is more, in keeping with the perceived role of Sulaiman the Magnificent, the "Red Sulphur" indicates a function that really belongs to the end of time.[211]

The loss of the heart of Sultan Sulaiman is equivalent to the loss of the Philosopher's Stone, or of the Grail[212]. René Guénon explains this state of affairs: "The loss of the Grail, or of any of its symbolic equivalents, amounts to the loss of tradition, along with all that it conveys; but in fact it is more true to say that the tradition is hidden rather than lost, or at least that it can be lost only

---

[209] Guénon identifies this principle with the "primordial legislator" Manu (ibid.), which is in turn reflected in Sulaiman's title of the "Lawgiver." The coincidence between Manu and -man (the Latin -mannus) may be noted.

[210] This saying is presented as the epigraph to Claude Addas' biography of the saint, and in fact provides her work with its title, *Quest for the Red Sulphur*.

[211] Abd ar-Razzâq Yahyâ (Charles-André Gilis), *La Petite fille de neuf ans, suivi d'une étude sur "le soufre rouge,"* Paris: Le Turban Noir, 2006.

[212] This is true even though the Grail's function as a container often obscures the perception of what it contains. Similarly, the purpose of Paracelsus' pommel is to serve as a physical container for the Philosopher's Stone.

to certain secondary spiritual centers that have ceased to maintain a direct contact with the supreme center."[213] In Aachen, emperors were enthroned between the thermal springs and the light of the Sun, but no longer. The "secondary spiritual center" of Turbék, a literal Heart of Europe modeled upon the supreme Heart of the World, no longer exists.

Concerning the hiddenness of tradition, however, it is worth recalling Paracelsus' teaching on the prophet Elijah or Elias:[214]

> Many arts are withheld from us because we have not ingratiated ourselves to God so that he would make them manifest to us. To make iron into copper is not as much as to make it into gold. Hence what is less God has allowed to emerge. What is more is still hidden up to the time of the arts of Elias when he will come.[215]

In the context of Elias revealing what is hidden, it is no doubt significant that he has an association with the summer solstice, at least through his relationship with Saint John the Baptist whose feast falls at that time of year.[216] The solstitial alignment between Constantinople and Aachen was the setting of the unifying promise of the 16th century, when Ottoman civilization was in its fullness; but its identity as the "Kizil Elma Alignment" long remained hidden. Even in the absence of the Ottomans, the appearance of the Virgin Mary at the heart

---

[213] *The King of the World*, op. cit., page 29.
[214] Followers of Paracelsus speculated on the close similarity between the name of Elias and the word for salt (*salia*).
[215] Quotation in Walter Pagel, "The Paracelsian Elias Artista and the Alchemical Tradition," *Medizinhistorisches Journal*, Franz Steiner Verlag, 1981, page 7. Paracelsus refers here to the transmutative power of a mineral spring in Hungary.
[216] Cf. *Sacred Geography and the Paths of the Sun*, page 112.

of the alignment provided a glimpse of its importance, given the Virgin's unifying role for Christianity and Islam.

Much more recently, a spiritual renewal of sorts has appeared near the western end of the alignment. In 1995, a modest dervish lodge was established in the Eifel mountains near Aachen, and its close proximity to the Kizil Elma Alignment seems far from accidental. The name of the lodge, the Osmanische Herberge, testifies to an Ottoman identity, and though the German master of the lodge belongs to the Naqshbandi Order, the Halveti Order figures in his lineage.[217] Beyond the regular practice of "sacred chant" (*dhikr*) at the lodge, its master is moreover a classical musician, and an organizer of "Sufi music" festivals at this harmonious location.

Nevertheless, the prophecy of the Red Apple has not yet come to pass. Until now, the caliphal relics remain preserved in Istanbul, where it is believed that they will yet be claimed by the Mahdi, the "Caliph of Allah" whose "Eliatic function" in preparing the return of Jesus is clear.[218] Archaeologists may specialize in revealing what is hidden, but they do so without regard for what is sacred. For now, the heart of the caliph is being withheld.[219] Even so, the search for it alone is no doubt an important sign of the times.

---

[217] Cf. Shaykh Muhammad Hisham Kabbani, *The Naqshbandi Sufi Way: History and Guidebook of the Saints of the Golden Chain*, Chicago: Kazi, 1995, page 335.
[218] Cf. Leo Schaya, "The Eliatic Function," *Studies in Comparative Religion*, Winter-Spring 1999.
[219] The institution of the caliphate was lost in 1924.

∇

The Place of Ivan Aguéli

The year 2021/1442 brought the publication of several books on the subject of the artist Ivan Aguéli, or rather the Shaykh `Abdul-Hadi `Aqili, whose role as a link in the initiatory life of René Guénon, or Shaykh `Abdul-Wahid Yahya, is of the utmost importance. Regarding the volume edited by Mark Sedgwick[220], caution must be called for, given the editor's distortions that were sufficiently demonstrated in his *Against the Modern World*. Still, we are fortunate to have a sudden outpouring of English translations of some of Aguéli's writings, both in the above volume and in Oliver Fotros' *Sensation of Eternity*. The latter is but a companion volume, however, to Fotros' other work, *The Pearl upon the Crown*, in which he presents his rather bizarre argument that René Guénon selfishly stole from the work of his predecessor Aguéli. Fotros does provide, however, some rather remarkable insights into the link between Guénon and his predecessor, even if he seeks to enlist them to support his case against Guénon.

Appropriately, Fotros can do no better than to quote from Guénon's successor, Michel Vâlsan, on the

---

[220] *Anarchist, Artist, Sufi: The Politics, Painting, and Esotericism of Ivan Aguéli*, London: Bloomsbury, 2021.

117

خادم الأولیاء الشیخ عبدالهادي عقیلی

Self-portrait and signature[221] of "Servant of the Saints, the Shaykh `Abdul-Hadi `Aqili"

---

[221] Reproduced from *The Pearl Upon the Crown*, page 103.

work of Aguéli: "René Guénon's readers will easily recognize some of the fundamental theses of his (Aguéli's) work, which will thus appear once again, not as the creation of an original individuality and syncretic thought, but as the development of a providential idea whose organs of expression and application were multiple and certainly will be until the intended purpose is achieved, to the very extent that it must be achieved."[222] Fotros begins his argument with Aguéli's translation "Supreme Identity" for the Arabic *wahdat ul-wujud*, a term subsequently adopted by Guénon who did not credit his source. Now, "Supreme Identity" refers to a singular summit of spiritual realization localized in the heart, and there is certainly no greater "providential idea" that may account for the unity in multiple "organs of expression." Yet rather than perceive this Supreme Identity beyond the individualities of Aguéli and Guénon, Fotros prefers to speculate on the motivations of the latter's personal identity.

There are, however, indications of this Supreme Identity even in the individual personalities of the two shaykhs. Ivan Aguéli was born John Agelii in Sweden in 1869 but changed the spelling of his name some 20 years after, with his surname altered to suit French orthography in keeping with his relocation to Paris. When this name is separated into the syllables A-gué-li, it is at least curious that the middle word "gué"[223] also happens to be the first syllable of the name Guénon. Of course this is a coincidence, but it is a remarkable one, given that the name Guénon is also somewhat unusual. Its other syllable is again a word – "non" – that serves to negate, and its presence here seems appropriate, given the author's negation of his own personality in his affirmation of the Primordial Tradition. Remarkably, if the "gué" in Aguéli is in turn negated, we are left with the

---

[222] Quoted by Fotros on page 90.
[223] "Gué" in French signifies the ford of a river.

letters A-li, that is, the English spelling of the name of the principal authority of Islamic esoterism.[224] As such, the Shah-i Mardan `Ali bin Abi Talib is properly understood as an embodiment of the Supreme Identity.

It might be countered that the A in Aguéli corresponds to the Arabic Ālif rather than the `Ayn that is the first letter of `Ali. Fortunately, when Aguéli signed his name in Arabic, he included his surname, a somewhat unusual practice (page 118); Guénon, for example, did not. Aguéli presents his surname as `Aqīli, and remarkably does in fact begin its spelling with an `Ayn. That is not all: the letters of the name `Ali correspond to the numerical value of 110 (70+30+10) in Arabic gematria; if the numerical value of the letters in the name `Aqīlī are added together, the result is 220 (70+100+10+30+10), that is, the first multiple of 110. Here we have, then, a simple calculation suggesting that it is none other than the principal authority of Islamic esoterism that may be understood in this providential example to have multiple organs of expression. While in Egypt, Shaykh `Abdul-Hadi's instrument of expression was the publication entitled "Il Convito/Al-Nadi," while the principal invocation in Islam addressed to the Shah-i Mardan is called "Nadi `Ali." For his part, and in keeping with his "self-negation" or spiritual poverty (*faqr*), Shaykh `Abdul-Wahid Yahya was known to direct seekers who came to him to the guidance of another, the Shaykh al-`Alawi, whose title "al-`Alawi" specifies the spiritual authority of `Ali.[225]

---

[224] The case of the Naqshbandi order is often offered as an example of a *tariqah* not deriving from the authority of `Ali, but this is misleading. Since this authority belongs to the Naqshbandi order through the master Ja`far as-Sadiq, it should rather be offered that the authority of Abu Bakr is absent from all other orders.

[225] In his book on the Shaykh al-`Alawi, *A Sufi Saint of the Twentieth Century* (Berkeley: University of California Press, 1973), Martin Lings does not explore the uniqueness of this title.

The Place of Ivan Aguéli

The occasion for the meeting of Ivan Aguéli and René Guénon was the establishment of the Akbariyyah, a group that the former had dedicated specifically to the Shaykh al-Akbar Muhyiddin Ibn `Arabi. The only context for this group belongs to a particular place, Paris, and a particular time, 1912. The Sufi initiation of Guénon is traced to this group, and so it is worth recalling Aguéli's teaching concerning two distinct types of initiation:

> The first is conveyed in established and recognised sanctuaries, under the direction of a living, authorized Shaykh (Guru) who holds the keys of mystery. Such is the "*Talimur rijal,*" the instruction of men. The other is "*Talimur-rabbani,*" or Divine or lordly instruction, which I allow myself to refer to as the "Marian initiation," because it was the one received by the Holy Virgin, mother of Jesus, son of Mary. There is always a master, though he may be absent, unknown, or even deceased many centuries before. In this initiation, you draw in the present from the same spiritual substance that others drew from in antiquity. This is rather frequent in Europe – at least in its inferior degrees...[226]

Because of the second initiatory type, this doctrine allows that the reality of Guénon's instruction must remain

---

It is perhaps worth noting that he chooses instead to relate that `Ali is "sometimes described as 'the St John of Islam'," (page 65), given that both Aguéli and Guénon were named after Saint John or Yahya.

[226] From "Pages dedicated to Mercury," presented in *Sensation of Eternity*, page 42.

incomprehensible to researchers like Sedgwick.[227] Of course, this type of initiation is well known in Sufism as the "*uwaysi*" transmission,[228] and so Aguéli's invention of the term "Marian" is significant here. No doubt it is worth recalling that Paris, where the Akbariyyah had its brief appearance, is positioned amongst the arrangement of cathedrals dedicated to *Notre Dame* the Virgin Mary and within the terrestrial projection of the constellation Virgo, as I have addressed elsewhere.[229] Aguéli may very well be indicating here the sacred predisposition of the place chosen to accomplish a "lordly instruction."

∇

Despite Guénon's noteworthy reticence concerning Aguéli – a matter of annoyance for Oliver Fotros – Guénon did in fact draw attention specifically to the name of his initiator. Sedgwick refers to this in his contribution to the aforementioned volume: "he wrote to a collaborator in 1938 that Aguéli was 'born in Sweden, or more precisely in Finland, but he was of Tartar origin,' and that his original name was probably 'Aquileff' or

---

[227] After more than a century, it has become abundantly clear that the Divine instruction in the works of Shaykh `Abdul-Wahid Yahya and those of his inheritor Valsân, Shaykh Mustafa `Abdul-`Aziz, has its proper source in Shaykh Muhyiddin. Though Valsân had many students, including Denis Gril and Michel Chodkiewicz, his principal inheritor is Charles-André Gilis, Shaykh `Abdur-Razzaq Yahya, whose works present overwhelming evidence of this source.

[228] The *uwaysi* initiation is a hallmark of the Naqshbandi Order in particular, and so it is worth noting the use of the term "*rabbani*" among the titles of contemporary masters of that order.

[229] See "The Labyrinth of the Age of Gold."

'Aguillef.'"²³⁰ Sedgwick is very quick to explain Guénon's apparent error concerning European geography, and ridicules Guénon's supposed attempt to rationalize the contradiction of a Swedish Muslim! Assuming that "probably" here signals a non-essential detail, it is worth reconsidering the shaykh's principal claim, that Aguéli was of Tatar origin through Finland. In the 19th century, there was indeed established in Finland rather than Sweden a noteworthy minority of Tatars from Russian lands, and it is very likely this fact that is most relevant, though it escapes Sedgwick's condescending view. Of course, Aguéli's own decision to change his name to "Ivan" indicates a particular orientation towards a Russian milieu that supports Guénon's indication here.

According to the Ottoman authority Evilya Çelebi, the Tatars of "Muscovy" received Islam through the holy example of Sari Saltik, and for Hasluck in his *Christianity and Islam Under the Sultans*, the widespread fame of this saint was a legacy of the Tatars. The veneration of Sari Saltik became a particularity of Sufism in the Ottoman Europe, along with an attachment to the patronage of the Shah-i Mardan. In the legendary account of his life, the *Saltikname*, Sari Saltik is a direct descendant of `Ali and inherits his sword and horse. Beyond this, Evliya Çelebi relates the most celebrated detail of his hagiography, that upon his passing, his body miraculously appeared in seven coffins that were then distributed to various locations in Europe; and the case of these seven tombs provides a most interesting parallel to the example of the Shah-i Mardan, to whom is attributed seven tombs throughout Central Asia.²³¹ In a general sense, the locations of the seven tombs of Sari Saltik may be found on the map of Europe, with one notable exception: a place rendered as "Yivançe"²³² reportedly in

---

²³⁰ Page 167.
²³¹ Cf. *Sacred Geography and the Paths of the Sun*.
²³² Unfortunately, Hammer-Purgstall renders the location as "Bívánjah" in his *Narrative of Travels in Europe, Asia, and Africa in*

Sweden. Remarkably, since this transcription would seem to be meaningless in Swedish, we are left with the simple interpretation that "Place of Ivan" is meant.

To appreciate the relevance of a link between the Swedish Ivan Aguéli and the Tatar saint, it may be recalled that an early source for the history of Sari Saltik, Ibn Battuta, relates that "things are told of him that are reproved by the Divine Law." We must therefore consider a most relevant subject that concerns Aguéli specifically, the path of the Malamatiyyah or "People of Blame." One of Shaykh `Abdul-Hadi's most important contributions was his presentation of Sulami's "Principles on the Malamatiyyah,"[233] and this contribution clarifies that the true representatives of this path may be misunderstood not because they violate the Divine Law, but rather because their preoccupations belong to a superior order.[234] For Aguéli, this path was not merely of doctrinal interest. According to Oliver Fotros:

> Aguéli very much identified with the Malâmatiyyah and wished to reconstitute its doctrines in the West. In fact, he even stated that the conversion of René Guénon to Islam was partly due to his inclination (*"maylan"*) towards the Malâmati path.[235]

Appropriately, Fotros cautions against passing judgment on Aguéli because of this spiritual affiliation, and so it is very strange that the author refuses to extend the same

---

the Seventeenth Century, apparently due to the error of a single diacritical point.

[233] Shaykh `Abdul-Wahid quotes at length from `Abdul-Hadi's work for his article, "The 'Popular' Mask."

[234] On the distinction between true and false Malamatis, as well as how the Divine Law stands as the first of the Four Gateways, see *Mysteries of Dune*, especially chapter 6.

[235] *Sensation of Eternity*, page 84.

courtesy to Guénon. Clearly, the personal example of Shaykh `Abdul-Wahid Yahya accords with the demands of the People of Blame, for whom every pretension belonging to the individual personality must be negated; and if he extended this attitude to the Shaykh `Abdul-Hadi, it only serves to confirm his understanding of the latter's spiritual identity.

In his introduction to Sulami's treatise, `Abdul-Hadi himself makes the following assertion: "In times of hardship, it is a Malâmati tradition to take shelter amongst the *Naqshabandiyyah* and the *Bektashiyyah*."[236] Such is indeed the example of Sari Saltik, since his tombs have been historically under the auspices of the latter order, but also the former, especially following the disbandment of the Janissaries in 1826. As far as the Law is concerned, the Ottoman *seyhü'l-islam* Ebu's Su'ud Effendi in the 16th century sought to account for the Malâmati identity of Sari Saltik by describing him as a Christian monk.[237] Of course, Ivan Aguéli was a painter by vocation, and it could be insisted that there is no more Christian art than painting, as the importance of icon painting within traditional Christianity demonstrates. There are more relevant parallels, however, to be observed between the Swedish painter and the Tatar saint. For example, the wanderings of Ivan Aguéli as far as Ceylon might easily be compared with the far-reaching adventures of Sari Saltik. There is also the strange matter of violence in Evliya Çelebi's account of Sari Saltik, the details of which are no doubt subtle and needn't distract us here, except in general comparison with the strange affair of Aguéli shooting a banderillero in protest of bullfighting in France.[238]

---

[236] Ibid., page 87.
[237] Cf. *Sacred Geography and the Paths of the Sun*, page 62.
[238] For the violence attributed to Sari Saltik, see ibid., pages 62-4; Aguéli's defense of the bull might further be compared with Saint Michael's defense of the bull at Mount Gargano (ibid., page 36).

If the Swedish painter of Tatar origin may be compared to the Tatar saint with a tomb in Sweden, we must not forget that *"maqam"* may refer in Arabic to the location of a tomb as well as to a spiritual rank or type. According to Ivan Aguéli, the "Marian" or *uwaysi* initiation was in his time "rather frequent in Europe," and since the master in such cases may have been "deceased many centuries before," the spirituality of Sari Saltik need not be discounted from Aguéli's own experience. Indeed, the current "discovery" of Ivan Aguéli, at least in English, appears to indicate a new manifestation related to the "Place of Ivan." Evliya Çelebi explained that Sari Saltik's tombs were multiple in order that the search for them "would produce everywhere a pilgrimage of Muslims and, from the pilgrimage, would result in the incorporation of these lands into the kingdom of Islam." Obviously the search for the Swedish *maqam* was abandoned long ago; yet Ivan Aguéli came from Sweden nevertheless to find Islam, and in this he was followed by René Guénon whose influence became incomparable. Aguéli was the first to identify "Islamophobia" as such, apparently, and because of it, both writers made recourse to a multiplicity of traditional expressions. There is no doubt, however, that for Aguéli and Guénon alike, their bond with the Supreme Identity was through their attachment to Islam. At the same time, it must be admitted that Islam was at the heart of Aguéli's role as the "Light of the North" (*nūr ash-shimāl*), as well as of Guénon's elucidation of the Primordial Tradition, with its comparably northern or "Hyperborean" character.

If the reality of the People of Blame seems difficult to reconcile with the Divine Law, so must this reality be even more incomprehensible to modern viewpoints, academic or not. Concerning the evaluation of the saints and those guided by them, modern authors would do well to consider a traditional perspective. For the civilization of the Ottomans, whose power in Europe followed upon the adventures of Sari Saltik, and for whom Ivan Aguéli was once thought to be an agent, the Shaykh al-Akbar was a patron saint. This judgment was issued concerning him:

> These books contain some material the content and expression of which is clear and understandable to all. Other material is veiled and kept secret from the eyes of people who only see the exterior of things…The ones who do not understand some things, distort them. Those who cannot understand these refinements should remain silent. They certainly should not accuse the writer of their own misinterpretations.[239]

---

[239] From the edict passed by Kemal Pashazade, translated by Shaykh Tosun Bayrak al-Jerrahi al-Helveti in Ibn `Arabi, *Divine Governance of the Human Kingdom*, Louisville: Fons Vitae, 1997, page xviii.

Other writings by Mahmoud Shelton:

Introduction to
Husayn Wā`iz Kāshifī Sabzawārī's
The Royal Book of Spiritual Chivalry
(Futūwat nāmah-yi sultānī)
Kazi Publications
2000

Alchemy in Middle-earth:
The Significance of J.R.R. Tolkien's The Lord of the Rings
Temple of Justice Books
2003

Preface to
Shaykh Muhammad Hisham Kabbani's
The Sufi Science of Self-Realization:
A Guide to the Seventeen Ruinous Traits, the Ten Steps to
Discipleship and the Six Realities of the Heart
Fons Vitae
2006

The Red and the White:
Perspectives on America and the Primordial Tradition
Temple of Justice Books
2019

Mysteries of Dune:
Sufism, Psychedelics, and the Prediction of Frank Herbert
Temple of Justice Books
2020

Sacred Geography and the Paths of the Sun
Temple of Justice Books
2021

www.ingramcontent.com/pod-product-compliance
Lightning Source LLC
Chambersburg PA
CBHW050030090426
42735CB00021B/3440